Realizing Your God Given Talents

By
Georgetta Marshall

PublishAmerica
Baltimore

© 2003 by Georgetta Marshall.
All rights reserved. No part of this book may be reproduced, stored in a retrieval system, or transmitted in any form or by any means without the prior written permission of the publishers, except by a reviewer who may quote brief passages in a review to be printed in a newspaper, magazine, or journal.

First printing

ISBN: 1-4137-0069-1
PUBLISHED BY PUBLISHAMERICA, LLLP
www.publishamerica.com
Baltimore

Printed in the United States of America

Dedication

I dedicate this book to my husband Robert and to my sons DeWayne and Robert II, whom I love with all my heart.

I pray that the words herein, will help you to find the very thing that God has given you to do.
You are my inspiration and the driving force behind a lot of what I do.

Acknowledgements

First and foremost, I want to thank my lord and savior, Jesus Christ for allowing me to be the vessel in which this message would flow through.

I send a special thank you to PublishAmerica for giving me the opportunity and privilege to allow my voice to be heard.

I thank my husband, Robert, who is my right arm, for being patient with me while I was spending long hours writing.

A great big thank you to Pastor William Hunter Crews, whom through his preaching helped to inspire me to begin the process of finding my talents.

I would like to thank Pastor Everett N. Jennings for his teaching Ministry that pushed me to reach for something bigger than myself.

Thank you first lady Barbara Jennings for your kind words of encouragement.

Thank you Maureen Ellington for being my picture-taking partner and for allowing me to use a portion of your life to get a point across in my book.

Also, I send a special thank you to Minister Althea Simpson, Dell Sanders and Paula Dawson for their wisdom and insight and all others who helped to make this book a reality.

Preface

I woke up one day– *smack dab,* in what appeared to be, the middle of my life. One can only assume where they are at, knowing that life can be gone in an instant. As my mind gave me a quick mental synopsis, I thought about all of the things that I said I would do. *You know the average story; I am going to buy a house, get married, and have children by the time I am thirty; I will be a multimillionaire by thirty-five, and travel around the world by the time I am forty.*

Where had all the time gone so fast? I wished I could chase time down with my current level of maturity and say, "Wait a minute. Time. Rewind back to the time when I entered into the wrong profession. Hold it! Give me another chance at this thing. I know what to do now."

Aging has a way of giving you a reality slap right in the face.

I had managed to snag the top technical and highest paying non-management position at the telephone company. However, my heart yearned for a great event that would bring me out of this job. I desperately wanted to leave it behind. I tried to imagine how I had ended up there in the first place. Sometimes, working there was similar to seeing a dog and cat fight, but with people. Each was fighting to either hold their ground or to move up the corporate ladder, through management. Once they reached the management side of the house, making others lives miserable seemed to be a pastime and a prerequisite for many.

Although, I knew that I was helping people with their telecommunication needs, there was a longing in my spirit to do the things that I felt God had really intended for my life. Somehow, I just knew that this was not it. Little did I know, God was about to begin that process by enlightening my mind through His Word and by showing me exactly what I needed to be doing.

On my quest to find my special niche in life, I noticed that it was the most tragic and stressful events that caused the real changes in me. When these changes did occur, they came like a loud drum beating into the very depths of my soul. They awakened every fiber of my being. Life flashed before my eyes as if it was just about to be taken away or dramatically changed. Then, suddenly I realized how precious moments were. The sound of birds chirping became important. Basking in all the glory of God's creations warmed my heart like nothing else, as I looked for meaning in my life. I exhaled and suddenly discovered the person called self. Then, it dawned on me that every event, job, contact, up, down, in, out, good and bad that I had ever encountered happened to me to bring me to this very point in my life. Whoa! What a journey it has been.

It is my prayer that if you are searching for your God given talents, that you will find within these pages the spark that lights the flame to your brighter tomorrow. With the Lord's guidance, I hope to help you discover what God gave us all at birth, our God given talents.

Introduction

Where are you and what are you doing with your life right now? Are you using the true talents that God has given to you? I ask the question because this very moment, right here and right now is all that you can really be sure of. If life ended now for you, how would your life read? Would you have left the beautiful imprints on the minds and hearts of all those that you touched with your God given talents? Would you still be drifting through life and searching for your gifts or would you be a quickly fading memory because you did nothing with your talents outside of you, yourself and I? Perhaps, at this present time, you are living out someone else's dream, possibly a parent's dream. Maybe you know what your talents are, but they are being used in the wrong way. Come and go with me down a rich path of discovery where you will find the treasures of your life.

CONTENTS

... *page*

I
Self Discovery... 16-21

When God Made Wonderful You
Genetics, The Key To Your Uniqueness
Your Special Abilities, Gifts And Talents

II
Identifying... 21-31

What Is A Talent?
A Look At What We Had All Along...
Now Is A Better Time Than Any...
The Greatest One...
Getting Focused In The Midst Of Confusion...
Taking The Right Road...
Sweet Beginnings....
Go For The Gusto-Think Big...
Distracted But Not Defeated...
Conceive It. Then Achieve It...

III
Preparation... 32-37

Perfecting Your Talent
Knowledge Is Power-Choosing A College
Cha Ching Others Will Pay Your Way
Method To The Madness

IV
Utilization ... 37-58

Sowing The Seeds Of Your Talents
Rewards
God Given Talents In Action-Using Your Talents
Fearless Fireman
Peacekeeping Policeman
Nurturing Nurses
Caring Cooks
Articulate Artists
Conscientious Cosmetologist
Affectionate Actor Or Actress
Teaching Talk Show Host
Ambitious Athlete
Working Writer
Searching Scientist
Tireless Teachers
Using your Talents In The Right Way

V
Ingredients For Success ... 58-63

Love, The Main Ingredient
Energy, A Vital Source Of Your Success
Money Sources-Taking Your Talents To New Heights

IV
Final Instruction ... 63-70

Jack-Of-All-Trades And A Master At Nothing.
Keeping Your Eye On The Prize
Saying Thank You

I
SELF DISCOVERY

When God Made Wonderful You

"God broke the mold when he made you," was a familiar funny saying amongst jokers when I was growing up. While many associated this saying with your physical appearance, it was also people's way of stating that you were so different that there was no one else on earth like you. Although, they were being facetious, in a sense, they were right. There is no one else on earth exactly like you. Each of us, are alike, but yet so different.

Think about it. Something that is one of a kind, whether it has life or is a mere material object, dazzles in it's own uniqueness. It makes a bold stand in all of its' own splendor. Take a material object such as a tailor made suit for example, it has its moments of glory, too. Cut and made to fit the person that it was designed especially for, the suit drapes that body in perfection. However, there is nothing more fascinating than the human race, equipped with its vast and complex inner and outer workings. As we all know, each body part has different functions that compliment each other and is necessary for the vitality of the whole body. Every person from the top of their head to the soles of the feet out to the tips of those one of a kind set of fingerprints, are wonderfully different. Nothing on earth can be compared or matches up to man's greatness. The human race is God's greatest creation. I do not think that our human minds can even comprehend what God did when he made man and woman.

So God created man in his own image, in the image of God created he him: male and female created he them. (Genesis 1; 27)

And the lord, God, caused a deep sleep to fall over Adam, and he slept: and he took one of his ribs, and closed up the flesh instead thereof; 22 And the rib, which the lord, God, had taken from man, made he a woman, and brought her unto the man. 23 And Adam said, this is now bone of my bones, and flesh of my flesh: she shall be called woman, because she was taken out of man. (Genesis 2; 21-23)

I became excited and filled with joy just thinking about the power of God while writing this book. When God made us, He gave us everything we needed to be different, but we keep trying to mimic each other in everything we do. Then, we penalize others for not being the same as we are.

Genetics, The Key To Your Uniqueness

Genetics, the scientific study of heredity and the passing on of characteristics of living organisms from one generation to the next, determines a lot. Genes, the basic units of heredity, are present in the cells of all organisms. Each cell in the human body has about 40,000 genes, which determine overall body build and traits such as eye, hair, and skin color. Although each family member passes down traits that are similar, many members of the same family also have widely differing features. There are even some differences in identical twins. Your genetic make up is different from anyone else's in the world. I say all of this to say, you are one-of-a-kind, feel it, know it, and embellish it!

Your Special Abilities, Gifts and Talents

Along with our genes, each of us, have our own special abilities, gifts and talents. These talents are as numerous as the stars in the sky.

Have you ever really thought about why one person is excellent at a particular thing while another may not be so good at that same thing? I grew up with, what had to be one of the world's best cooks. My mother's friend, Mrs. Covington, was born in Kentucky, but has lived in California for as long as I can remember.

REALIZING YOUR GOD GIVEN TALENTS

In my mind, I can still see her welcoming smile. The beautiful gray streaks in her hair complemented her Carmel toned skin.

Her home had a nice country down-home feel to it. You could smell and feel the love that she had for cooking. She literally fed most of the neighborhood children. Sometimes she fed us breakfast and dinner. When the word got out that she was cooking a particular meal, it traveled like news in the daily newspaper. Her mouth-watering meals drew in a multitude of people. I never saw her turn anyone away. She was one who could make simple eggs taste like a fine gourmet meal. Her specialty gumbo and her famous Mexican dishes were delicacies.

I am sure that we can all think of someone whose cooking skills are not up to par and never will be. Some of us would not have to look beyond ourselves to find that person. The burnt smells coming from the kitchen, the strange tastes in the food, and the bricks that were called cookies have all been the proof in the pudding. Cooking may not be your cup of tea, but you can be sure that there is something that is.

For the sake of those who feel that anything can be learned, let's just say that this was true. However, if you try forcing those things that simply do not fit with you, wouldn't you feel just like that same baby who has managed to master lockjaw games, when it comes to eating those green peas? Trying to force-feed a talent into your life that is not meant for you will stand out like a sore thumb. Now there are some things that we simply must try to learn anyhow for the sake of survival. Cooking would be one of those things unless you are blessed enough to have someone cooking for you every day of the week. Therefore, if you know that cooking is not your talent, then don't go and try opening up a restaurant that will feature your cooking. I spoke of Mrs. Covington's cooking talent simply because it seems to be one of the things that she loves and lives for. Why not allow the main talent that you display to others, be the talent that you love and live for too.

Anyhow, these differences are the very things that give us our individuality. It is how God made us. Your uniqueness means there are no carbon copies of you.

Sometimes it is not an easy task to see your own talents; so listen closely to the compliments and comments of others. You must take some time now and focus on yourself. Pay special attention to your likes and dislikes. Search out your gifts and abilities. Look for what makes you happy above anything else. On this road to self-discovery, focus your thoughts on all the things that God supplied you with. Stop and make a list of them right now.

Things That I Love To Do

_____
_____
_____
_____
_____
_____
_____
_____
_____
_____

When you look in the mirror what do you see? Through Christ Jesus, you should see the wonderful image of you looking back. You should see the love in your eyes that God has instructed you to share with others. The look of concern, eager to help those in need, should be on your face. You should see beautiful lips that love to spread the word of God. You should see splendid, magnificent, delightful, incredible you.

Prayer

> *Dear Lord,*
> *Help me to learn the history of my great*

beginning, so that I will know where I should go. Help me to appreciate who I am and each individual characteristic that you gave to only me. Allow my eyes to see my own unique beauty inside and out. Teach me to love myself in such a way that it would flow over to other people. Thank you dear Lord for creating me.
   Amen.

II
IDENTIFYING

What Is A Talent

Talents are the natural endowments of a person, a characteristic feature, aptitude, or disposition of a person, general intelligence or mental power, special often creative and artistic aptitude and ability. Talents can also be defined as a unit of weight or money, but our main focus here will be on the natural abilities that God has given each and every one of us. Think about these descriptions of a talent and try to identify immediately what you think some of your attributes are. They are not hidden.

A Look At What We Had All Along

We don't have to look far to identify our talents. During our early childhood, our talents present themselves like white flags surrendering in battle. Our friends and families have complimented us on them repeatedly. Teachers have worked to bring our talents to the forefront as early as elementary school. It is here, within these early days of our lives that we begin self-discovery. As we grow and learn about ourselves, our talents flow out of us with ease because we naturally become good at them. They are gifts from God. These talents are the things that we love and live for. Also, they are things that we enjoy doing just for the sake of doing them. Our talents are our own special niches that we have to contribute to life. If you have watched and listened, you may already know what your talents are, if not, they have yet to be discovered.

Now Is A Better Time Than Any

Whether you are a child, a teenager approaching adulthood or a senior in search of something more, now is a great time to identify your God given talents and put them to good use. I am a firm believer that if you are old enough to start reading and deciphering things about life, you are old enough to start discovering your talents. In fact, that time is when it should all begin. However, if you are up in age and still have strength and life in your body, it is definitely not too late. Unfortunately, we do not give children enough credit for what they can comprehend as early as age two. Then, we try to bury the seniors before their time. It is God who will have the final say on who does what and for how long.

I had the pleasure of attending a program at the St Joseph's Tabernacle in Detroit, Michigan, titled, "What Talents Have God Given You." The program featured mainly young children as young as age two. Each of them demonstrated what they believed to be their talent. Watching the adults preparing these young people to discover early on what God has blessed them with, was a sight to behold. There is nothing like seeing a two year old reciting the Lord's Prayer. It warms the heart.

I have tons of respect for the unsung gray-haired heroes who have raised scores of children and grandchildren in some cases, but continue to press on in life reaching for that next talent to love someone with. They are resilient angels which whom we should get a lot of our wisdom from.

The Greatest One

Most people have many talents, but there is usually one that stands out from the rest. The greatest talent has shown up when you're sitting in the pews of a church and there is not a dry eye in the place after a singer has sung from the very depths of her soul. You know she was born to sing. Great talents show up when an eloquent and effective speaker captures the attention of his or her audience and has them hanging on to every word. Lives will be changed. The best talents show up on the test papers of students when a teacher has given them their all and all. Knowledge has been passed on. If you are saying to yourself, "I would clear a room if I sung a song, the entire first row would be sleeping during my speech and my nerves would be shot in a classroom," keep your mind open to other possibilities these are obviously not your talents. There are endless ways in which great talents show up. I have seen them present everywhere from kitchen tables to backyard gardens. Whenever or wherever these God given talents show up, you will know them by their grand style entrance. Intricately placed in your life at a given point in time, they edify the spirit. Upon their conclusion, they graciously exit, leaving wonderful memoirs of having been there. It's like licking that good cake mix that remains in the bowl after the batter has been poured into a cake pan.

Getting Focused In The Midst Of Confusion

If you are confused about what a God given talent looks like and find yourself in a place that exploits, demoralizes or is illegal, please know that this is not your God given talent. Being the middleman in Pookie's stolen TV and bootleg VCR ring does make you an accessory to the crime. When talents are God given, you will not have to wonder if you're doing the right thing, you will feel and know that you are. The very essence of that talent will spell goodness. The Holy Spirit or some like to think of it as that little inner voice, will convict your conscious when you are doing wrong and make you feel guilty. On the other hand, do not forget about that other inner voice that will try to justify every wrong. You must ignore it. Do what is right at all cost. Righteousness prevails in the end.

GEORGETTA MARSHALL

Taking The Right Road

If you have ever known anyone who went off to college for many years of study, only to find out years down the road that they pursued the wrong thing, then you know how important it is to identify your true talents early.

Getting off to a wrong start is not an unlikely event. With all of the people in our lives who try to pull us in every direction possible, no wonder we get sidetracked. Unfortunately, this pulling starts at a very young age. We are pretty much coached into what others think we should be.

Dad may want you to become that lawyer that he always dreamed of being. Mom may want you to make your career in the family floral shop. Sister may think you're gorgeous looking and want you to become a model.

Images of frustrated little girls being paraded across a stage in the name of beauty, to fulfill a parent's missed dream, still cloud my mind. Behind all the lace, barrettes, bows and patent leather is an unhappy child.

Listen closely, and you can still hear the echo of an angry father screaming from the bleachers at little Johnny for striking out. His frustration is driven by the fact that he wants his kid to become what he never could be. Fun has flown south and no one is benefiting. Unfortunately, this coaching does not stop at childhood. Many of us are coached clear through high school and right up to college graduation on what someone else thought we should be. Sometimes, parents have the best intentions in mind. They may choose what seems like a very rewarding field for a child to go into in hopes of securing the best life for that child. My friend Maureen told me about how from the time her grandson Chris was Three years old she had groomed him to become an astronaut. Every summer he would attend the summer camp at NASA, which cost her $500 every time. Through the years, a great amount of time, effort and money was spent preparing Chris's life for this great career. Although, Chris had always dreamed of being an astronaut, his real love and talent was art. He could draw extremely well at a very young age and spent much time doing so. Then, one day in Chris's eleventh grade year, after all that preparing, he brought home a term paper that he had written titled, "Do I Follow My Life Long Dream And Make My Parents Happy Or My God Given Talent?" His paper was so compelling that after Maureen read it, with tears in her eyes she politely told him to follow his God given talent.

The natural human side of us, want to be crowd pleasers. We long for everyone to love and accept us. On our quest to be people pleasers, should we allow others to live out their missed dreams through us? Should we be looking for what God's purpose is or people's purpose is for our life?

Sweet Beginnings

Where do we begin our quest for what our life holds for us? There are many scriptures in the Bible that point us in the direction of God first. The blinking caution signs are there in our minds, telling us over and over, God first, God first, put God first, but are we listening? A person trying to figure out their life without first looking toward their origin, which is the word of God, is like a flower trying to grow without dirt, water and sunshine.

But seek ye first the kingdom of God, and his righteousness; and all these things shall be added unto you. (Matthew 6: 33)

Get wisdom, get understanding: forget it not; neither decline from the words of my mouth. Wisdom is the principal thing; therefore get wisdom: and with all thy getting get understanding. (Proverbs 4: 5 & 7)

The wisdom of God is the word of God. Wisdom is the main ingredient, but wisdom without understanding is no good. Do not confuse wisdom with education. There are a lot of educated people with no wisdom or as some would say educated fools. Gaining wisdom and understanding allows us to see all that our life should be. With wisdom, we can look within ourselves and see the beauty that God so delicately placed inside each and every one of us. In that beauty, lie's our talent. Many of us do not even realize that the beauty is there until we study God's word. That is when we find out that we are children of a king and crafted by design by God almighty. In the midst of our search for Gods wisdom, we should be going to the Lord in prayer and asking for understanding and guidance.

Ask, and it shall be given you; seek, and ye shall find; knock, and it shall be opened unto you: For every one that asketh receiveth; and he that seeketh findeth; and to him that knocketh it shall be opened. (Matthew 7: 7-8)

Although you may have identified what you think your talents are, pray anyhow and wait on the answer. Let the Lord direct your path.

Trust in the lord with all thine heart; and lean not unto thine own understanding. (Proverbs 3:5)

Prayer

> *Dear Lord,*
> *I ask, in the precious name of Jesus, for you to teach me to seek you first. Help me to identify everything special that you put inside of me to use. Reveal to me my God given talents. Bring my talents to the forefront of my life where they can be plainly seen. For I know that once they are brought to light, then I can use them to bring glory unto your kingdom. Thank you dear lord, for all of these blessings. In Jesus name I pray.*
> *Amen.*

REALIZING YOUR GOD GIVEN TALENTS

Go For The Gusto-Think Big

We all desire to have a certain kind of lifestyle. Nobody wants to struggle to pay for basic living expenses. On top of being able to pay our bills, we want to look good and live well. What do we do if the one talent that we love and know is our talent, barely pays enough to make ends meet? We have to look at all the possibilities that our talents could have. For example, if a schoolteacher was not happy with the current rate of pay by the school board, couldn't that teacher also teach by writing books and lecturing? I have seen people in the medical field advertising health remedies and people in law enforcement marketing safety devices. With creativity, you can bring a special twist to any talent or special abilities that you have. We should not confine ourselves, and our talents, as one would confine something in a cardboard box. Life is full of endless possibilities. The only boundaries are the ones that we set within our own minds. Think big. With God, all things are possible.

Distracted But Not Defeated

There are many reasons why a person may not realize their God given talents early on in life. You may have always known what made you happy and exactly what you wanted to do since childhood. Somewhere down the road, someone probably either told you directly or made you feel like your talent was not good enough. They may have told you how you were following a pipe dream and you believed them. You developed a limited view of yourself. So, here you are, still searching.

Many of our lives, simply put, are being pulled in too many directions. We allow a lot of things to occupy our time, but sometimes not intentionally. Many women, like I did, find themselves suddenly in three or four different roles such as, wife, mother and worker, leaving little or no room for personal development. During the early years of my marriage, I can remember feeling frustrated because I felt like everybody in the world was accomplishing something but me. Many family and friends had gone to college and started successful careers. As time went by, God showed me how, at that particular time in my life, that I was doing my life's most important job and that was being the best wife and mother that I could be. Therefore, I used all of my talents on them. That is why after the diapers, bottles, kindergarden, parent-teacher conferences, junior high school, proms, home-coming, high school, graduation and everything else in between, we arrive back to the place where it all begin and say, "Ok, where was I?" Oftentimes, these are the reasons why we see so many women develop new interests after they have raised children, because now there is more time for self-development.

Many men, also, are too busy working hard and providing for their families to capture the true essence of the talent that they were meant to develop. A lot of men have the calluses, bruises and gray hairs to prove it. If you cannot find daily quiet time to yourself to pray and put into perspective, those things that concern your life, you are much too busy.

Enough cannot be said about planning. Through Christ Jesus, have a plan and work that plan, otherwise, you leave yourself open for any old thing that comes along. Your life becomes an unguided path. A person without plans often reminds me of a person that has gotten on a boat headed out to sea, but instead of steering the boat, they sit back and relax and say, "Oh, let me see where the wind will take me." I know that this sounds totally ridiculous, but when you have no plans, what are you saying to your life? Ask yourself that question. Even though things will not always go as planned, planning adds direction. It gives us an intended target and target date. Planning gives you something to shoot for and something to look forward to.

Another reason why many of us do not realize our talents is because we pursue money first. Money talks and is a true motivator for most people. The mighty dollar has deterred many from their true talent. This is why we have so many people, who are miserable in their current positions. They followed the dollar instead of their true talents. However, I have seen people take the simplest of talents that they love, and make fortunes with them. While we are out beating the pavement for that next pay level in that corporate establishment, our true answer may lie within those untouched God given talents. Am I telling you to quit your corporate job? No. What I am saying is to use the job as a stepping-stone to realize your true talents. Then, use your true talents to do the things that will glorify God. By doing so, you will bring purpose and direction to your life. The emptiness you once felt will be replaced with satisfaction. Then, if it is God's will and your desire to leave that job, by all means do so, especially if it is causing you great discomfort. Life is too short to work 30 miserable years before you can retire.

Fear, another thing that causes people to miss the mark, is a true crippler. It paralyzes a person into a particular state, causing them to be afraid of the unknown. Fear of failing and of being ridiculed, are high on the list of fears. Oftentimes, friends and family are the very ones that put us down. We stagger from their innuendoes. As motivational speaker, Les Brown says, "do not allow someone else's negative opinion of you to become your reality." What does Gods word say about fear?

For God hath not given us the spirit of fear; but of power, and of love, and of a sound mind.
(II Timothy 1: 7)

But I will forewarn you whom ye shall fear: Fear him, which after he hath killed hath power to cast into hell; yea, I say unto you, Fear him.
(Luke 12: 5)

Fear not, little flock: for it is your Father's good pleasure to give you the kingdom.
(Luke 12: 32)

God has told us exactly who to fear. If we remember God's Word and listen to good and constructive criticism and discard the rest, we can weather the storm of criticism and fear.

I can honestly say, for all of these reasons and others, it took me longer than I would have liked it to, to realize and utilize my talents. New plans were often in the making, but they were not the right plans. I thought that if I could just have a lot of money that would fill the void that I felt inside. I needed a purpose, something that would really make my life worth living. When life cautioned me to turn right, I usually turned left. I was good at making that good idea a reality, but often stopped in mid-stream. From my experiences, I learned that when you are trying to capture a talent that is not meant for you, the sizzle will cool fast. Thank God, that through His Word, I finally got it right. Whatever situation your life finds you in, allow your talent to shine right where you are until the winding road of life gets you to the place where you really want to be.

Conceive It. Then Achieve It

Like a seed, an idea is planted within the mind. It is watered with visions of how it will be reached. Thoughts of this idea becoming a reality play over and over in the mind. No man has achieved anything without dreaming it up in his mind first and then believing that this thing could come to pass. It is called faith.

Now faith is the substance of things hoped for, the evidence of things not seen.
(Hebrews 11: 1)

Faith is, believing in the things that we cannot see.

I have literally had people tell me that they do not believe in anything that they cannot see. Everyone at some point and time has to rely on faith. When we lie down at night, we go to sleep having faith that we will rise in the morning. We simply cannot see what the morning will bring ahead of time. Only God has that kind of power. When we leave our homes, headed for work in the morning, we have to have faith that we will return safely in the evening. There are certain circumstances that man does not have control over. In situations such as these, we have no choice but to have faith.

We also need to have faith when bringing our hopes and dreams to reality by way of our God given talents. We need to have faith and believe that those very talents are ours to develop and use. Yes, God has given you a mind, which stores a vast amount of information, a body that is unlike anyone else's on earth, a soul that should be saved and rein in heaven and an array of wonderful talents to develop and use to be a blessing to yourself and others.

There are people who choose not to see the greatness in every person. Do not let these dream snatchers, make you believe that your talents are not yours. They roam about looking for someone to devour. People who cannot see anything for themselves, more than likely, will never see anything for you.

I have spent a lifetime admiring and being blessed by people's God given talents consciously and unconsciously. I have taken great joy in seeing people reach insurmountable heights, with their talents, and with the most humble beginnings. For this reason and others, it is a pleasure and privilege to write on the subject of God given talents.

Whatever mountain you are trying to climb have the faith that you will get over the top and you will. Conceive it and you shall achieve it. Believe in God. Believe in yourself. Remember garbage in garbage out. Whatever a man thinks in his mind that he shall be. The great Napoleon Hill, an author, said it all in this title alone, *Think And Grow Rich*. Think and grow rich in the talents God has given unto you.

As you can see, identifying your talents is the first crucial step. If you do not get the identifying part right, your life could be off on a tangent for a while. However, once you have identified your true talents, you will be well on your way to being a blessing to yourself and others. It is no secret that what you possess, already lie's within you. It has been there with you all along. Now expose it and get ready to prepare it for the world to see.

III
PREPARATION

Perfecting Your Talent

Be ye therefore perfect, even as your father which is in heaven, is perfect.
(Matthew 5: 48)

Once you have identified your talents through self-analysis, God's wisdom, which consisted of the word of God, and prayer, take the next step. It has been said that education is the foundation and one of the keys to success. Therefore, we should get the necessary training to perfect what God has already given us the inclination and ability to do.

Knowledge Is Power- Choosing A College

I hope by now you have identified at least one of your talents, preferably your main talent, and have prayed for guidance and direction. Oftentimes a certificate, degree, license or some form of training is required to perfect your talent. There are a host of colleges, universities and other training institutes where you can acquire this education.

Do not despair, many authors have paved the way to choosing a college or higher educational institution. There are numerous books that give their pick of the best schools. *America's Best Christian Colleges* and *The Student Guide To America's 100 Best College Buys* are just two of the many books on the market. See table 1.1 and 1.2 for college sources in all fifty states at the back of this book.

Check your local libraries for books on choosing a college or higher educational institution. The library, the most valuable free book source, is often overlooked. If you cannot find the titles that you are looking for, ask a librarian to check other branches. Books can be sent to the branch that is closest to your home. If the library does not have what you need, then check your local bookstores. Make a list of the schools you're interested in, then, contact the schools for more information.

Christian Schools

A Christian based education can bring much to those in search of their God given talents. These institutions provide students with a good Christian foundation and education. Many focus on preparing men and women academically and spiritually to serve Christ Jesus in their careers. I like what Dr. Roger Parrott, President of Belhaven College, said at his annual address of 2001, "Contentment is not found in a career, but in our calling, which includes understanding and enjoying our Godly gifts, building on the qualities of our temperament and capturing the focus of our motivation."

Traditional Schools

The traditional colleges and universities are other good sources for perfecting your talents. Many uphold high academic standards and provide the best education that money can buy. Realizing the complexity of each student's life, educators have added many options. There are weekend and evening college programs, accelerated degree programs and classes on the Internet. I took an Internet course and found it to be quite interesting. Everything was done online. I even ordered the books for the class online. Education has come a long way. Embrace it.

On The Job Training

Your training may not always come in a formal school setting. For instance, a singer may have been trained by singing in the shower or in front of family and friends. Many cooks perfect their talents right from the kitchens of their own homes. Debbi Fields perfected her famous cookies right in her own home. As a young mother with no business experience, she started her business, Mrs. Fields, in 1977. She now has stores all across the country. A basketball player may have started out polishing his skills at the neighborhood recreation center, which ultimately took him all the way to the NBA.

Correspondence Courses

Informal training may also come by way of correspondence courses. These train at home programs sometimes come complete with a personal computer. These courses are self-paced programs that allow students to earn training or a certificate or degree in the privacy of their own homes. The student is given books and a course outline of all the dates and assignments that are to be completed. The class may meet only 2 to 3 times. The books and/or tapes in some cases become your teacher as you independently complete the assigned work.

Seminars

Another source of informal training is seminars. They will usually last anywhere from a few hours to several days. These seminars are jammed packed with information, but are usually sponsored in order to convince you to buy a particular course, program or product. Do your research before attending the seminar. You will be better equipped to determine if what they are offering is good or bad.

Cha Ching Others Will Pay Your Way

Paying for your education can be easier than you think. There are more programs than ever before that will pay for your education. Your local library and bookstore carry books on financial assistance that list the various programs, requirements and deadlines. You can also apply for assistance at any college or university.

REALIZING YOUR GOD GIVEN TALENTS

Grants

Grants are free money sources that will pay for the cost of your education. Our federal government offer's numerous grants. Funding Your Education, an introductory publication for students not yet enrolled in a post secondary school, provides general information about the U.S. Department Of Education's federal student financial aid programs and how to apply for them. This publication is free. Write or call the Federal Student Aid Information Center.
Federal Student Aid Information Center
P.O. Box 84
Washington, DC 20044-0084
(800) 433-3243

Scholarships

Scholarships are another source of free money. There are numerous schools, businesses and organizations that award scholarships. The award could be for a certain dollar amount. It could also be a two-year or four-year degree scholarship. Some schools give scholarships for academics, while others may award an athletic hopeful a scholarship to play basketball or football. Still, others may receive scholarships based on artistic ability.

Employee Tuition Assistance

Check with your employer, many have tuition assistance programs as well. Employers are now seeing the importance of education and are reaping the benefits from better-educated employees. In fact, many employers are picking up the entire tab including books and registration fees. Some employers even offer classes right on site.

Loans

Loans are available for your use. The borrower must repay the loan. Therefore, you should not apply for a loan until you have exhausted all of the grant, scholarship, and other free money sources that you can get your hands on. There are extra fees such as interest added on to what you are borrowing. Lastly, why weigh yourself down at the start of realizing your talents with unnecessary debt. Somebody will get all of these free money sources available. Why not you? Use loans as a last resort.

Method To The Madness

One might ask, "If it is a God given talent, why do I need to perfect it?" There are rules and regulations that society has established to protect everyone. If you had been interested in the human body all of your life and wanted to be a brain surgeon, you would require many years of training to gain the expertise. A degree and a medical license would be required to practice this profession in a hospital legally. Likewise, a person who wants to be a nurse's aid may have always had a gentle caring spirit and a knack for taking care of others, but need the certificate to utilize these gifts in a nursing home setting. Would you want your uncle, who feels that because he has a love for the mouth, that it gives him the right to practice pulling some of your teeth, without having been to dental school? I would think not. Therefore, every talent at some point needs fine-tuning to make it better or legal to practice in our society.

Once you have found your method of training, whatever industry your talent falls in, find out everything that you can about that industry. Read everything that you can get your hands on relating to your talent.

As you can see, there are many ways of getting the education that is needed. Whatever your talent is, get the necessary training. Prepare, prepare and then prepare again. Whether your training comes from a Christian college, a traditional training program, correspondence or the Internet, get the best education that you can. Don't short change yourself. Practice and nurture your gifts whenever you are given the opportunity, for with each opportunity comes a chance to spread love, glorify God and showcase to the world what the Lord has given to you.

Prayer

Dear Lord,
Prepare me to prepare myself for the training that is needed and often required to be successful. Let my mind be sharp and focused. Help me to retain all the knowledge that will be acquired. Lord, wrap your arms around me in those classrooms where intimidation can come so easily. I will be sure to give you all of the praise and glory. Thank you Lord.
Amen.

IV
UTILIZATION

Sowing The Seeds Of Your Talents

I can remember when I was a young girl first learning to swim. Even though they said the water in the pool was heated, I always walked up to the edge of the pool and stuck my big toe in before jumping in. It was my way of testing the waters.

Putting yourself and your talents out there is kind of like putting your big toe in the water. You have identified your talent and have gotten the necessary training to polish it and make it better. Now you are ready to show the world what you can do.

You can possess the best talents in the world, but if you never show others what you can do, what good are they? Start by telling people what you can do. There are many ways to get the word out:

    Business cards
    Fliers

Newspaper ads
　　　The Internet
　　　Radio and television ads
　　　Family and friends
　　　By word-of-mouth

Use as many of these avenues as possible. Take the time to examine all of the areas that the seeds of your talent can be planted in.

Rewards

There are some rewards to sowing. The average person does not want to do something for nothing. Whether it is a job that we are doing or a good deed, the natural human response is to want something tangible for our work. In other words, when we plant the seed, we want to reap the harvest.

The harvest can come in many forms. If we perform work, we want the harvest of compensation. If we do a good deed, we may want the harvest of appreciation and admiration from others. The more seeds that are planted, the more harvest there will be. We should know that without seed time there is no harvest.

We all have something to sow into the world. It is a big melting pot integrated with all shades of people, different ethnicities, beliefs, sizes, shapes and talents.

Sometimes I like to think of the world as the ultimate people fruit salad with an array of beautiful colors and tastes. However, the salad is not without its bad apples. Nevertheless, we must sow in the lives of these bad apples too. We must sow God's word, our time, and talents on them in hope that they may turn their ear unto the Lord and reap the harvest of eternal life.

We must sow goodness in all the places that we go. The seed must be scattered even in unfruitful soil. The seed will sometimes fall on deaf ears, but sow anyway because someone else nearby may be listening. Our job is to plant the seed. It is God who brings the harvest.

REALIZING YOUR GOD GIVEN TALENTS

If you have sown discord, strife, bitterness and deceit, get ready to reap the same things back. There is no way around this. Therefore, we should treat people the way that we would like to be treated. Then, sowing the good seeds of your talents will reap you the rewards of a lifetime.

God Given Talents In Action -Using Your Talents

Neglect not the gift that is in thee... (1 Timothy 4: 14)

After you have identified your talent and have gotten the necessary training, how will you use your talent? For as many talents as there are, there is an equal number of ways for using your talents to help people and glorify God. During our lives, we are often told to make good use of something, whether it's time, money or a talent.

As a young adult, my big sister taught me how to grocery shop and get the most for my money. She told me to plan my meals and shop for the items that would be needed to prepare each meal. At that time, money was hard to come by. I usually planned for meals that called for hamburger; such as spaghetti and chili, because I knew that we could eat off of these meals for a couple of days. Although, those days are long gone and may seem trivial, I learned how to plan and make good use of the little money that I had. It was good practice for one day making good use of a lot of other things in my life. Open your eyes now and take a good look at all the talents that are being used in our society that a lot of us take for granted. Gain an appreciation for how each one gives us something we either need or just want.

Fearless Fireman

For God hath not given us the spirit of fear; but of power, and of love, and of a sound mind. (II Timothy 1:7)

At the young tender age of ten, one might ask a young boy what he would like to be when he grows up. He confidently says, "I want to be a fireman."

As one watched him go about his daily life, already you can see the characteristics of a fireman developing in his personality. He ran to the rescue of a younger sister, who had fallen off of her bicycle and lay crying on the sidewalk. He helped his grandmother with all the things she could no longer do very well for herself. At the time, no one thought very much of these little events. Time passed and before they knew it, he stood before them strapped in all the gear of a fireman.

On September 11, 2001, he raced to disaster not knowing what lay ahead. Courage filled the air, as he stormed into the burning World Trade Center building to save lives, knowing that he may not make it out alive.

Certainly, this is a God given love and courage that he possessed. One might ask, what kind of person would risk his life everyday in this manner? We must remember that we do not choose everything that we want to do. God gives specific tasks and talents to specific people, who simply accept them.

America will never forget the firemen who risked or gave their very lives so courageously during the September 11 tragedies. The horrific scenes of the planes crashing into the twin towers of the World Trade Center building, causing them to collapse, will be forever etched in our minds.

The memories of the gapping hole that was put in the Pentagon and the crash site in Pennsylvania will forever serve as harsh reminders of how precious life is. In the midst of it all, let us focus momentarily on what the firemen's job consisted of and how they helped our communities long before September 11.

Every year, fires destroy thousands of lives and property worth millions of dollars. Firefighters are helping to protect the public against this danger. Firefighting is among the most hazardous occupations. The risk of death or injury from the sudden cave-in of floors or toppling walls and danger from exposure to flames and smoke, poisonous, flammable and explosive gases and chemicals are some of the things firefighters are faced with.

Because firefighters must be prepared to respond to and handle any emergency that arises, organization and teamwork is required. At every fire, firefighters perform specific duties assigned by a company officer. Some of the assigned duties would be connecting hose lines to hydrants, positioning ladders, or operating pumps. A firefighter's duties may change several times while the company is in action. Therefore, they must be skilled in many different firefighting activities such as rescue, ventilation, and salvage. Some firefighters operate emergency rescue vehicles and fireboats. They also help people to safety and administer first aid.

Fire prevention is another responsibility that the fire departments must handle. Specially trained personnel inspect public buildings for conditions that might cause a fire. They may check the number and working condition of fire escapes and doors, building plans, the storage of flammable materials, and other potential hazards. In addition, firefighters educate the public about safety and fire prevention. They frequently speak on this subject before school assemblies and in our communities.

Along with their extensive duties, firefighters have stringent working conditions. The fire stations are usually equipped with facilities for sleeping and dining because of the long hours the firefighter must spend at the station. When a fire alarm comes in, regardless of the hour or weather conditions, firefighters must respond quickly.

The fire department provides a valuable public service to our communities. It is sometimes in the midst of tragedy where we learn to appreciate what has been afforded to us all along. Our hats go off to all firefighters.

Peacekeeping Policeman

Blessed are the peacemakers: for they shall be called the children of God.
(Matthew 5: 9)

Police Officers, another vital link in our communities, fundamental purpose is crime prevention through law enforcement. They perform this with their day-to-day patrol activities. They patrol assigned sectors in motor vehicles or on foot, working alone or with a partner, paying close attention to area conditions and inhabitants.

The job of a police officer brings to mind the biblical scripture *Daniel 3: 8-30*, where Shadrach, Meshach and Abed-nego were thrown into the fiery furnace for not bowing down and worshiping the golden image. They all walked out of a fiery furnace without a scratch on them. With the risk of danger around every corner, police officers go into the fiery furnaces called neighborhoods daily to serve and protect, but sometimes they don't come out. Faced with every kind of situation imaginable, they help to protect the law-abiding citizens. They strive to rid our cities of crime and drugs and many lose their lives trying.

Along with their duties, police officers still manage to devote time to the Police Athletic League (PAL). PAL is a recreation oriented juvenile crime prevention program. The program relies heavily on athletics and recreational activities to tighten the bond between police officers and kids in the community. Through this bond, the league hopes to reach children early enough to develop a strong, positive attitude towards police officers in their journey through life towards the goal of adulthood and citizenship. There is a great need for PAL, because a lot of our young people do not respect police authority. Many are unruly, disrespectful and down right dangerous. Although nationally known as a recreation program, the Police Athletic League also offer programs such as computer skills, mentoring, and homework help, to further aid our children.

I often think about the word of God and how it polices our lives the same way the policeman polices the streets. The Word helps us to get the junk out of our lives. We then can go forth and live better lives.

In spite of police protection, many of us may feel that our communities are still just as chaotic as ever. While many of our communities may need more police presence in the neighborhoods, we can all help out by keeping our eyes and ears open to suspicious activity. Notify the police of any criminal activity that you see. Things are at an all time low in our society, when people will stand by and watch someone being hurt or even killed and never even alert the police. Think about if we did not have policemen at all, our communities would really be in trouble. We need policemen to keep the peace and are forever indebted to them for the valuable service that they provide.

Nurturing Nurses

Let no one seek his own, but each one the others well-being. (1 Corinthians 10:24)

If you have ever been sick in a hospital, then you have had nurses who were genuinely concerned about nursing you back to good health. The nurse softened the blow of your illness with her good bedside manner. Intrigued by the rarity of her goodness, upon your discharge from the hospital, you thanked her. She responded with, "You're welcome, but I was only doing my job." Little does she know she was also doing the Lord's work by spreading goodness?

God instructs us to help each other. Goodness shows up when a person is working where they should be. They take great pride in what they do. People feel good when they can be treated like a person instead of patient number fifty-one in bed A. It is nice to know that there are still modern-day Florence Nightingales.

Registered Nurses (R.N.) observe, assess, and record symptoms, reactions, progress and administer medications. They assist in convalescence and rehabilitation and instruct patients and their families in properly caring for the patient. In addition, nurses help individuals and groups take steps to improve or maintain their health. In hospitals, nurses work closely with physicians carrying out their prescribed regimen of treatment for the patient.

Many nurses prefer to work elsewhere instead of in a hospital setting. Therefore, they explore all of the other areas of nursing. There are nursing home nurses, public health nurses, private duty nurses, office nurses and occupational health and industrial nurses.

If nursing is your talent, take your love, stamina and your incredible emotional stability to deal with human suffering, and nurture all that you can. Your love may be the last love that a person sees as they make the transition from life to death. For more information about the nursing field contact the:

American Nurses Association,
600 Maryland Avenue, SW Suite 100 West,
Washington, DC 20024
(202) 651-7000,
1 800 274-4ANA (4262)
or contact nursingworld.org

Caring Cooks

It is written man shall not live by bread alone, but by every word that proceedeth out of the mouth of God. (Matthew 4: 4)

It does not matter if you are a mother or grandmother who cooks for a family or a gourmet chef who prepares meals in one of the finest restaurants in the world; people are drawn together by your meals. Your ability to tantalize the taste buds has become an art form. The mouth-watering hot apple pies, the deliciously prepared southern fried chicken, and those creamy mashed potatoes with gravy are filled with your love for cooking. Just when you thought it could not get any better the aroma of piping hot buttered homemade rolls fills the air.

These grand food finales have become the center stage of social events, family reunions, weddings, parties, church events and love filled gatherings. Food has brought people together and helped to mend broken hearts and relationships. During these gatherings, make God's Word a part of your menu. Tell your guests that the body should crave God's Word just like the body craves food. Some creative ways to share scripture lessons at your table is with decorative napkins or centerpieces imprinted with scripture. It will be a blessing to have fed your guest spiritually as well as physically.

We have cooks that show their talents in a wide variety of restaurants that line the streets of every city under the sun. Whatever your desires are, they are there to satisfy your appetite.

Southern California has some of the best Mexican food cooks in the world. With Southern California having a large Hispanic population, the number of Mexican food restaurants has soared. If you are craving burritos, tacos, enchiladas, tamales, and quesadillas, you can find them there. Many establishments make their own tortillas and have their own special blends of beef, chicken and pork fillings.

Are you looking for the best steak and cheese sandwich ever? I was told that it resides in Philadelphia, Pennsylvania. Philadelphia is home of the Philly steak and cheese sandwich. It has been said that this mouth watering succulent ultimate sandwich is something to be reckoned with.

Turn on the television and you may be able to catch *Emeril Live* whipping up something that looks delightful and delicious all while music is being played in the background. To every good cook who has ever tantalized a taste bud, *mmm...mmm* good. Keep up the good work. Bon appetite!

For information about the restaurant industry contact the National Restaurant Association: www.restaurant.org.

Articulate Artists

Whatsoever thy hand findeth to do, do it with thy might...
 (Ecclesiastes 9: 10)

Art, an event frozen in time, on paper, a canvas, or in clay, is truly a wonderful gift. Although, art comes in many forms, I am discussing that art which lines the walls, tables and mantles of our homes, art galleries, museums and businesses. The art can be an exquisite piece from a world-renowned artist, or an item from a newly found artist. However, within each piece of art, lies a story being told without words. Truly a language of its own, it has been said that each piece of art can say a thousand words.

If you have ever watched an artist in action, they draw, paint or sculpt these images with such ease. The natural way in which their hands move across the paper or clay bringing something to life right before your eyes is amazing. It seems like magic.

Each of us has a responsibility to bring into the world something beautiful. Displaying images of love, hope, peace and joy can only bring glory to God and more beauty to the world.

Metropolitan Museum of Art
http://www.metmuseum.org
New York (212) 879-5500

African American History Museum
(Largest of its kind)
315 E. Warren, Detroit, Michigan
(313) 494-5800

Cogswell Polytechnical College
Train to be a 3D modeler, animator, video game or web designer.
(800) 264-7955

Conscientious Cosmetologist

Favor is deceitful, and beauty is vain: but a woman that feareth the Lord, she shall be praised.
(Proverbs 31: 30)

Women have long been admired and sought after for their beauty and essence. Most women would agree that alot goes into keeping yourself beautiful and vibrant. Along with the proper diet, exercise and rest, there are people who specialize in making a person look beautiful.

REALIZING YOUR GOD GIVEN TALENTS

The cosmetologist is one who uses their crafty skills to sculpt beautiful hairstyles, nails and pedicures. However, their duties could also include makeup, eyebrows, body waxing and skin care. This weekly ritual has become a real treat for overworked women, looking to be pampered and revitalized. Everyone from housewives to corporate executives, desire this treatment.

The beautician is responsible for outer beauty treatment, but what things can the client do to work on inner beauty? While their client is seated in that comfortable chair, and receiving a wonderful hairstyle, nails and pedicure etc., they could just relax and meditate. By not allowing our appointments to become gossip sessions, we are in fact being rejuvenated inside and out, ultimately giving ourselves a total beauty package, while giving the beautician, who has heard it all, a break.

According to the National Accrediting Commission of Cosmetology Arts & Sciences (NACCAS), the salon industry continues to be a job-seekers market. Salon owners reported to NACCAS that they planned on filling 500,000 positions in the first six months of 1999 alone.

The beauty industry wants you so bad that ACE Grants are being given to help you start a career in cosmetology. The ACE Grant is being sponsored by three major beauty industry associations; the American Association of Cosmetology Schools (AACS), the Cosmetology Advancement Foundation (CAF), and the Beauty and Barber Supply Institute (BBSI). For information contact the AACS at 1 888 411-Grant.

Affectionate Actor Or Actress

Be not forgetful to entertain strangers: For thereby some have entertained angels unaware.
(Hebrews 13: 2)

An actor or actress takes a part and depicts a character with the goal of bringing its audience a story that will captivate and entertain.

If their job is being done, the audience will hang on to every word while awaiting the outcome. It is almost as if the actor has really become the character.

In my favorite classic movie, *The Ten Commandments*, did Charlton Heston not make you believe that he was really Moses? The special effects and the beautiful rich colors used in this film made me feel like I was standing right there at the Nile River.

I often wonder if these actors ever dreamed that their performances would be shown for decades. Could they have ever imagined that they would be enlightening people around the world and giving them a glimpse of what these biblical events might have really been like? While many have argued about the validity of this movie, I try to keep in mind that the majority of television programming is not accurate. The Bible is my true guide anyhow. Also, I think about the good things that people have gained from the television experience. *The Ten Commandments* certainly taught us that everyone and everything must obey God. In spite of the shortcomings, seeing some of the biblical events acted out on television really drives the message home.

Think about *Matthew 8:23-27* when Jesus was asleep in a boat with his disciples and a storm arose on the sea. His disciples became fearful and awoke Jesus fearing that they might perish. But he said to them, "Why are ye fearful, O you of little faith?" Then he arose and rebuked the winds and the sea, and there was a great calm. So the men marveled, saying, "who can this be, that even the winds and the sea obey him?" I love this passage. Who are we not to obey God, when even the winds and the sea obey him?

Many years have gone by and millions of award winning performances have been played out since this classic. By way of the big screen, Hollywood has brought us years of movies enveloped with life lessons. We have laughed and cried, sometimes all within the same scene. We have learned a lot. However, this has not been done without piles of distasteful movies.

It is my hope that actors and actresses will pick their parts in the same manner that they would responsibly pick a life partner. For if

REALIZING YOUR GOD GIVEN TALENTS

you have given an Oscar winning performance on pornography or some other degrading piece of work, what have you gained? Once this part is played out, there is no way to retract it from the minds and hearts of the people that have already been touched by it. Anybody can talk loud and say nothing. Therefore, give an award winning performance that will allow dignity to stand tall when the curtain comes down.

Those aspiring to become actors and actresses should become a member of the Screen Actors Guild. All major movie studios hire from this union. Write to: Screen Actors Guild, 5757 Wilshire Blvd., Los Angeles, CA 90036 Fax: (323) 549-6526 or email: jobs@sag.org

The top 5 agencies in Hollywood are:
Creative Artists Agency (CAA)
Literary and Talent agency
9830 Wilshire Boulevard
Beverly Hills, California 90212-1825
(310) 288-4545

William Morris Agency
Talent and Literary agency
One William Morris Place
Beverly Hills, California 90212
(310) 859-4000 fax (310) 859-4462

International Creative Management, Inc. (ICM)
8942 Wilshire Boulevard
Beverly Hills, California 90211
(310) 550-4000

United Talent Agency (UTA)
(310) 273-6700

Endeavor Talent Agency
(310) 248-2000

GEORGETTA MARSHALL

Teaching Talk Show Host

If any man speak, let him speak as the oracles of God; if any man minister, let him do it as of the ability which God giveth...
(I Peter 4: 11)

    Daytime TV talk show hosts, as controversial as they are, hold in their hands an incredible amount of power. They took America by storm when they first aired in the 1970's with their brow raising topics on anything imaginable. Now over three decades later, they are still going strong.

    In my opinion, no one does this in a more positive way than Oprah Winfrey. With each show, she graces the stage with her warm spirit and knowledge, bringing unto the world something that will help, motivate and up lift a person. Her angel network, remembering the spirit stories, inspiring topics, remedies to problems and love for the public, is just what America needs. In an arena all by herself, she has taken this very controversial stage, and turned it the largest help clinic imaginable. At the end of every show, people leave with something wonderful in hand and heart.

    Although, some of the other talk show hosts may use their platform for shear entertainment, the public still comes away with something. That something, most often, is to know that we don't want to be like the people on those shows and for some people that is enough. Clearly, there are problems with people in every arena, but we must recognize and lift up that which is good. We must give credit where credit is due.

Ambitious Athlete

Train up a child in the way he should go: and when he is old, he will not depart from it.
(Proverbs 22: 6)

REALIZING YOUR GOD GIVEN TALENTS

The athletically inclined person has much to offer. Their strength, drive, stamina and athletic ability can bring much to disadvantaged youth, who reside in areas that do not have enough or no recreational activities. These people could be elementary, Jr. high School or high school coaches, Olympic competitors, athletes, jocks or any other person with the athletic ability.

The quality time spent nurturing, protecting, and teaching, will remain with many of these young people the rest of their lives. For some, athletics could be the only real quality time they get. For others, it will be their only alternative to not ending up on drugs or in prison.

Yes, there is time to teach our youth Godly ways of being a team player right on those fields, baseball diamonds, basketball courts and the like by getting a little in here and there.

With many families being one-parent households or both parents working, young people are often left alone. There are sad reminders everywhere of what happens to youth who are left alone for too long. If you thought you could not make a difference with athletics, think again. Somebody made the difference with Venus and Serena, the world's best at tennis.

Studies have shown that between the hours of 3 p.m. and 8 p.m. crime rises, because it is the time when school-aged children are without supervision. During these hours, a lot of parents are working.

After school programs are needed to keep our young people busy with good things to do. These good things could include recreation and a host of other activities. As parents, we must do all that we can do to help our young people. Our future lies within their hands.

Team USAnet in a joint effort with Monster.com and the U.S. Olympic Committee's Athlete Services Division, will offer the first ever virtual athlete services center designed exclusively for U.S. Olympians and hopefuls to come. Contact one of these organizations for further information. U.S. Olympic Committee, locations: Colorado Springs, Colorado; Chula Vista, California and Lake Placid, New York. (719) 632-5551. Another contact would be, the Women's Sports Foundation in New York, at (800) 227-3988.

GEORGETTA MARSHALL

Working Writer

Commit thy works unto the lord, and thy thoughts shall be established.
(Proverbs 16: 3)

Books, the doorways to many places near and far, can take you anywhere imaginable. They teach, entertain, inform and test your mind. A book is no more than what is in our minds and hearts poured onto paper. The book of all books, the Bible, brings unto us the creation of the universe, everything in it and man, all the stories of the unsung hero's who were touched by the miracles of God during a time long before ours, instruction from God for daily living and his promises, the revelation of what is to be and much more. The Bible, God's word, is man's gateway to heaven.

For the aspiring writers and published authors, I challenge you to write what will help, edify, entertain and lift up the mind, heart and soul. Our world today needs love in every form.

In order to tell a story, get to a truth or bring about a life lesson, some writers bare all and bring about the worst scenarios to capture their audience. The responsibility of the reader is to not miss the message in the midst of all these tactics.

The written word is unique in that like art, it is events frozen in time, but with ink. It can be read and then put on a shelf, then taken down three years later to experience again. Remember a writer's words can remain long after they are gone, either glorifying or disgracing God. For those interested in writing, take a look at the following resources.

Book: *Writer's Market* or www.writersmarket.com. This book will give you contacts for literary agents, publishing opportunities, book publishers, contacts and much more.

Writing seminar: Middlebury College Bread Loaf Writers Conference in Vermont.

Finding a literary agent: *The Literary Market Place* (R.R. Bowker) or visit www.literarymarketplace.com.

Would you like to be a Christian screenwriter?
Contact ActOne:
Writing For Hollywood
1760 North Gower Street, Hollywood, CA., 90028
(323) 462-1348
or go to the Web site at: www.actoneprogram.com.

Reach for the stars.
Walt Disney Pictures And Television Fellowship wants writers.
500 Buena Vista Street, Burbank, California 91521
or call (818) 560-6894.

Searching Scientist

Ask, and it shall be given you; seek, and ye shall find; knock, and it shall be opened unto you. (Matthew 7:7)

Science has brought us down a path filled with scientific studies and technological advances. The knowledge obtained by scientists has many valuable uses in our society. It makes labor easier with new machines, processes, and materials. It brings aid to us with medications and treatments. It improves the food supply. Also, new sources of energy and raw materials are found with science.

Ecological crises such as damage to the ozone layer, acid rain and rising sea levels are identified and the effects that these conditions have on society can be studied. In addition, science contributes to our understanding of how people act in groups and how best to lead and govern people. As you can see, the areas of science are vast. Therefore, I would like to concentrate on two areas that I find fascinating, space exploration and medicine.

GEORGETTA MARSHALL

Space Exploration

Space exploration has taken place, because of our human curiosity about the earth, the moon, the planets, the sun and other stars, and the galaxies. Exploration of space has included piloted and un-piloted space vehicles, which have ventured far beyond the boundaries of the earth to gather valuable information about our universe.

Many of us can only dream of going into space like the pioneers Yuri Gagarin, a Soviet cosmonaut, John Glenn, Donald Slayton, Walter Schirra, L. Gordon Cooper, M. Scott Carpenter, Virgil Grissom, Alan Shepard, Neil Armstrong, Buzz Aldrin and Mae Jemison, the first Black astronaut and many others did. Their scientific studies have expanded our knowledge beyond earth. God gave these individuals impeccable courage to explore what he made and to give a report back to mankind. By way of satellite, books, newspapers, television and radio they gave their reports back. We have gained knowledge about how the sun, the planets, and the stars were formed. We now also have insight into whether life exists beyond our own world because of these great people. A wealth of information, on everything that was discovered during space explorations, is stored in our encyclopedias. With all of the past and recent tragedies of space exploration, let us all come together and pray for the families that lost loved ones. They will be remembered as the shooting stars of science. Time will only tell what further space studies will uncover.

For further information contact NASA's website, http://www.spaceflight.nasa.gov and www.nasajobs.nasa.gov/how_to_apply/application_forms.htm

Medicine

The miraculous discoveries made in medicine, absolutely baffles my mind. The next time you experience a headache or cough and you take a pain reliever or cough medicine, shortly after your problem subsides, think about how awesome that is. Who are these men and women who have studied the human body in medical laboratories so intensely that they have come up with cures to ailments and diseases of all types? The list is endless. Certainly God is at work here. Many of the surgical procedures, implants and transplants, that have been done successfully recently, are nothing short of remarkable. Time will only tell what other advances will be made in future studies. The things that tickle our imagination today may become a reality tomorrow. These great scientists would have never made it to where they are without God and the great educators placed in their lives.

Tireless Teachers

Preach the word! Be ready in season and out of season. Convince, rebuke, exhort, with all longsuffering and teaching.
(2 Timothy 4:2)

Educators, these overworked and underpaid champions, bring to us a wealth of knowledge. During the early years of our life, they help to shape and mold our very foundation. In elementary school, teachers help us to recognize and develop our God given talents. Society has not recognized them as a vital vein in our communities; otherwise their pay scales would reflect that of maybe a professional basketball or baseball player or more. In spite of the ills of society, teachers trudge on, educating and inspiring all who seek knowledge. Oftentimes, teachers who teach in the inner city public school systems, may teach in leaky run down dilapidated buildings of poorly ran districts. Nevertheless, they still give love and education to those who want to see their way up and out of poverty, while they themselves could be in somewhat of a similar situation.

Finally when that part of the education process is complete and a graduate is giving a commencement speech and reaches back to recognize a specific teacher, it is because that teacher was the one who lit the torch for him or her to carry to graduation day. By way of their God given talents, teachers are the reason for untold amounts of great people.

As you can see, there are many talents being used in every way imaginable. There were only twelve mentioned here and they touch our lives in countless ways. Sometimes, we just need to stop and really look at how good life is, in spite of all that we may be going through. Think about any special ability that a person possesses and you will see a God given talent. It would be impossible to list them all within the pages of this book. I touched on the particular ones listed here simply because they inspire me and we often forget how valuable they are. Whatever your God given talents are, whether they are mentioned within these pages or not, realize them today and use them to love, give, help, inspire, build, restore, lift up, teach, discover, feed, nurture, comfort, protect and to honor God. For, if we are not doing something to the glory of God, we are not doing anything.

Using Your Talents In The Right Way

What a tragic event it is to see a wonderful God given talent being used in a derogatory way or not being used at all.

I am often reminded of talents being wasted when I hear a perfectly good singing voice demoralizing women in the lyrics of its song. Often blasted from hi-fi car stereos and radio stations, the songs, depict women as being female dogs and weed-whackers. (B's and H's, if you know what I mean) What the listeners do not realize is that they are being unconsciously programmed to really believe what the songs are saying. Sing loud, but say something worthwhile. Unfortunately, our male counterparts are not alone.

Some women singers do not step out on stage without first pulling out all the stops. They make a sultry grand entrance on to the stage wearing their bedroom attire, roping the men in hook, line and sinker. They bring shame to the entire female gender with their elaborate lyrics that give details of a sexual and explicit encounter, leaving nothing for the imagination. We give T.M.I. or Too Much Information. Then, after we are exploited and used up, we try to justify what we have done with the paycheck.

REALIZING YOUR GOD GIVEN TALENTS

There are many other ways in which talents are not being used in the right way. When I see a person that is homeless and has resorted to pushing a grocery basket down the street, begging for change and sleeping on park benches, naturally my heart goes out to them. While being very careful to not be judgmental, I think about the limited view, the homeless person, had of themselves. I pray that God will help them see that there is so much more to their life. Realizing that life can take us down any road, I cannot help but to think about the un-used talents. It brings to mind the scripture, the parable of the talents.

> *For, the kingdom of heaven is as a man traveling into a far country, who called his own servants, and delivered unto them his goods. 15. And unto one he gave five talents, to another two, and to another one: to every man according to his several ability; and straightway took his journey. 16. Then he that had received the five talents went and traded with the same, and made them other five talents. 17. And likewise he that had received two, he also gained other two. 18. But he that had received one went and digged in the earth, and hid his lords money. 19. After a long time the lord of those servants cometh, and reckoneth with them. 20. And so he that had received five talents came and brought other five talents, saying lord, thou deliveredst unto me five talents; behold, I have gained beside them five talents more. 21. His lord said unto him, Well done, thou good and faithful servant; thou hast been faithful over a few things, I will make thee ruler over many things: enter thou into the joy of the lord. 22. He also that had received two talents came and said, lord, thou deliveredst unto me two talents: behold, I have gained two other talents beside them. 23. His lord said unto him, Well done, good and*

faithful servant; thou hast been faithful over a few things, I will make thee ruler over many things: enter thou into the joy of the lord. 24. Then he which had received the one talent came and said, lord, I knew thee that thou art an hard man, reaping where thou hast not sown, and gathering where thou hast not strawed: 25. And I was afraid, and went and hid thy talent in the earth: lo, there thou hast that is thine. 26. His lord answered and said unto him, Thou wicked and slothful servant, thou knewest that I reap where I sowed not, and gather where I have not strawed: 27. Thou oughtest therefore to have put my money to the exchangers, and then at my coming I should have received mine own with usury. 28. Take therefore the talent from him, and give it unto him which hath ten talents. 29. For unto every one that hath shall be given, and he shall have abundance: but from him that hath not shall be taken away even that which he hath. 30. And cast the unprofitable servant into outer darkness: there shall be weeping and gnashing of teeth.
(Matthew 25:14-30)

Although this scripture is talking about a monetary form of a talent, it is a great lesson on learning how to use what we are given. Remember the world and everything in it belongs to God. He has allowed us to be caretakers of all of his stuff. When God has given us something, we had better use it and in the right way or risk losing it. I cringe at the echoes of the, should have done, would have done, and what if cries of those who did absolutely nothing with their talents. I am glad that I woke up.

Prayer

Dear Lord,
Help me to use my God given talents in the right way. In our pursuit for money, fame and what we consider success, it is often so easy to get sucked into doing things that are not pleasing to you. Please Jesus, keep me from evil doings and keep evil doings away from me. Allow my talents to be used in such a way that it becomes someone's light in their dark world. Thank you for these blessings.
Amen.

V
INGREDIENTS FOR SUCCESS

Love, The Main Ingredient

This is my commandment, that ye love one another, as I have loved you.
(John 15: 12)

A recipe has many ingredients that are used to make an end product. Each ingredient is important and brings some flavor into the recipe. There is usually a main ingredient. If the main ingredient is not used, it will throw the entire recipe off. For instance, flour would be the main ingredient for a cake recipe. Without flour, it simply would not be a cake.

Like a recipe, our talents have certain ingredients that are needed for success. They need to be brought out of us with the proper identifying techniques. They need to be perfected with training. To top it off, they need the main ingredient, love. Use your talent to show love. Your talent mixed with love will make a wonderful end. If you are operating within your true talent, showing love with your talent will come easy, simply because you are doing what you adore. It should come easy, because God instructs us to love one another.

Using your talents without showing love is self-seeking, unfruitful to others, dull and lifeless. Without love added, your talents will dry up and die on the vine.

Love is more than just a warm and fuzzy feeling. It is more than the look of passion into another's eyes. It is quite more than the butterflies in the pit of the stomach. Believe me, it is much more than sweaty palms. Love is an action word. You must do something. That something should be a blessing to someone else's life.

Energy, A Vital Source Of Your Success

You will never realize, perfect and use your God given talents without the energy to do it with. You need physical energy to do anything. Our bodies crave the daily exercise and proper nutrition needed to function at their highest level. Lack of exercise and poor nutrition brings on obesity and health problems.

Studies done by the American Medical Association shows that obesity is now one of the leading causes of death over smoking. Studies also show that more Americans are overweight now than ever before. Eating too much food is unhealthy and we all do it at one time or another. It shows a lack of discipline within one's self. If we are to be good stewards over each other with our talents, then we certainly need to be good stewards over our own lives first.

Taking care of ourselves, should be at the top of our to do list, right under God. For we cannot take care of anyone else, whether it be husband, wife or children, until we take care of our self. It shows in our appearance when we do not keep ourselves together. Sluggishness, tiredness and laziness set in. Because we feel bad, we start to look bad. It kills the spirit of wanting to do anything.

Whatever miracle diet plan the world will bring to us next, please know that there is no substitute for plain old eating right and regular exercise. You cannot get a better plan. Starvation and regiment food plan diets are not the answer; believe me I have tried most of them. They take away vital foods that are needed by the body. After a period of time, your body is literally starving for certain foods. What a harsh way to treat God's body. He has informed us in His Word just what our bodies are to be. They are to be holy living temples for Jesus to reside in.

Sometimes, medical problems may cause obesity instead of overeating. There are medical conditions that cause weight gain and water retention. Regular check-ups with your physician are needed to stay abreast of what is happening to your body. By getting the proper nutrition, regular exercise, rest and check-ups by our doctor, then we are doing what we can to sustain good health for as long as we possibly can. Then, when our energy is gone, as it one-day will be, we can sigh with shear joy and know that we did everything that was physically possible while we could.

Money Sources-Taking Your Talents To New Heights

With God all things are possible. He tells us in His Word to ask for what we desire and that would include money. If we have not, it is because we ask not.

22: Have faith in God. 23: For verily I say unto you, that whosoever shall say unto this mountain, Be thou removed, and be thou cast into the sea; and shall not doubt in his heart, but shall believe that those things which he saith shall come to pass; he shall have whatsoever he saith. 24 Therefore I say unto you, what things so-ever ye desire, when ye pray, believe that ye receive them, and ye shall have them. 25 And when ye stand praying, forgive, if ye have ought against any; that your father also which is in heaven may forgive you your trespasses. 26 But if ye do not forgive, neither will your father which is in heaven forgive your trespasses. (Mark 11:22-26)

It is no secret that it takes money to be able to truly be a blessing and to reach the largest amount of people in need of your talent. No matter how small or insignificant you may think your talent is, there is someone somewhere that can be helped by it. Therefore, money for your talent may be needed. Talking about money is often a touchy subject with some people, but a much-needed resource on earth when trying to do anything. I used to feel guilty about desiring to have more of it. I soon learned that God wants us to enjoy the earthly possessions as well as the heavenly possessions that await us. I also realized that the more money I had, the more of a blessing I could be to others. Think about any charitable organization that feeds the hungry and helps the poor. They all need monetary donations to survive. Yes, these organizations need our support in a physical way, but it is the money that keeps them afloat.

You might decide to take your talent to another level. For example, a pharmacist, who worked in a popular pharmaceutical chain store now wants to open up her own drug store. Perhaps you are already in business locally, and want to soar by offering your services nationwide. It would take money to make these things happen.

Surely God knows what we are in need of before we ask. Through faith and prayer, your monetary sources can come to you in many ways.

Free Money

Start by looking for free monetary sources first. There are numerous grants available through the federal government and local agencies. The government give away millions of dollars every year in grant awards.

Employment

Money could come from your current job. There are ways that we could get some extra money right from our current jobs. Working overtime will provide some extra cash. Although, overtime is limited with some companies, it is still a good source if available. Also, if you have a company 401K Plan, you could borrow from yourself. The money is automatically deducted from your paycheck to repay the loan. Some companies will allow you to stretch those payments out over a four or five year period.

Savings

If you're blessed enough to have savings stored up in the bank, that would definitely be a viable and easily accessible source. However, I do not suggest emptying your savings account. You need to have cash on hand for emergencies or unforeseen circumstances that may arise.

Loans

Loans are readily available for those with decent credit. Banks, credit unions and other loan institutions often slash interests rates to get you to borrow money.

You may be able to come up with some other source for money that is not listed here. Pray, be creative, think positively, and let the driving force behind your desires get you the money that you need. We tend to forget that all that we have and all that we are is because of God who is in control of everything. Just ask; you just may receive.

VI
FINAL INSTRUCTION

Jack-Of-All-Trades And A Master At Nothing

Ladies, you can bring home the bacon, fry it up in a pan and never let your husband forget that he is the man. Your superwoman approach to life has you spread from the boardroom to the kindergarden classroom to your own personal endeavors.

Gentlemen, your do-all, be-all, attitude has made your ego soar to great heights, but have you spread yourself like a thin layer of butter? Everything from your handyman quick fixes to your technical tactfulness has helped many and has you looking like "the man."

You want it all at any cost.

In our quest to have our cake and eat it too, what lies ahead for the person, that is trying to be too much? Just as a rubber band will pop when stretched beyond its limits, so will a person that is trying to be everything. We will soon become tired and stressed from the pressure of trying to hold down too much for too long. We cannot possibly have and do it all.

There will be many things that will capture our interests. We will want to charge full steam ahead with doing them. However, we have to know our limits. There are many things to consider.

If you have a family, this will have to be taken into consideration. Family requires a lot of our time and attention. Somewhere in the rush hour of life, the family has been put on the back burner. We see the horrible consequences of it everyday. We have to change this by not pursuing more than we can handle.

Time is only going to allow for so much during any given day. Put your mind to one of your talents first and master it. Do not move on to anything else unless time allows for it. Remember, success is not measured by how many different talents we tackle, but how well we do with the one God given talent that was meant for us.

Keeping Your Eye On The Prize

Getting yourself to a state of being conscious about your life and staying focused on the end result is a task within itself but necessary to make good use of your life and talents. We need to remember the reasons why we are doing whatever it is that we are doing. Maybe your efforts will bring something special to someone's life. Perhaps the manifestation of your talents will change someone's life forever. Maybe your talent can one day provide a cure for a deadly disease. Whatever the significant change or impression is that you will make with your talent; your passion for what you do will be the driving force behind keeping your eye on the prize.

There will always be something that will try to take your life off of its course. This is just the way that life is. Life brings on many trials and tribulations. On a day-to-day or hour-by-hour basis for some, there are events unfolding that could take your life on a whirlwind spin. Life sometimes reminds me of a fight; just when you thought you were getting up from the last punch, here comes the knock out punch to try and finish you off. However, God is always there. He tells us just how to block those spiritual warfare blows that try to bring us to our knees.

Put on the whole armor of God, that ye may be able to stand against the wiles of the devil. 12 For we wrestle not against flesh and blood, but against principalities, against powers, against the rulers of the darkness of this world, against spiritual wickedness in high places. 13 Wherefore take unto you the whole Armour of God that ye may be able to withstand in the evil day, and having done all, to stand. 14 Stand therefore, having your lions girt about with truth, and having on the breastplate of righteousness; 15 And your feet shod with preparation of the gospel of peace; 16 Above all taking the shield of faith, wherewith ye shall be able to quench all the fiery darts of the wicked; 17 And take the helmet of salvation, and the sword of the spirit, which is the word of God; 18 Praying always with all prayer and supplication in the spirit, and watching thereunto with all perseverance and supplication for all saints. (Ephesians 6: 11-18)

Now, I know what this scripture really means. You really need to be grounded in the Word of God to weather life's storms. Read, study and meditate on God's Word for it is the only sure thing that will keep you conscious about your life, focused and sane.

Go to Genesis and see man's origins. Genesis clearly shows us where we came from therefore designing a path of where we must go. Travel through the Word and read about the covenants God made with Abraham, Isaac and Jacob and see that the covenant includes you too. Look at the task that God gave to Moses and know that you have one too, even if you have not realized it yet. You may not be leading thousands of Israelites out of bondage, but what you do will be just as important.

Let the psaltery sounds of Psalms heal you in your times of trouble, but do not stop there. Be thankful for the birth of Jesus and be inspired by all of the healings and miracles He performed throughout the land. Never forget the ultimate sacrifice Jesus paid with his life, in order that we might live. When you finally arrive at Revelation, allow it's content to stamp the mark of approval on your heart and know that hell is real.

Use your talents to stay focused. I find that writing helps me to stay focused. Nothing gives me a more visual picture of my thoughts and myself than keeping a journal. A journal provides self-talk, self-visualization, self-analysis and it's just one of the little handy tools I picked up from Oprah.

Keep your eye on the prize. The end result of the use of a talent could bring so many wonderful things, a saved life, cure for a disease, the hungry fed, a life lesson and so much more. What will be the end result of your talent? What kind of impact will you make on the world?

Saying Thank You

In every thing give thanks: for this is the will of God in Christ Jesus concerning you.
(1 Thessalonians 5: 18)

You are at the pinnacle of your success. You have managed to become that great person that you dreamed of one day becoming. The curtain is drawn. All eyes are on you. The crowds go wild. You are shaking with excitement. The crowd quiets down as you walk up to the podium to say a few words. Clinching the microphone too tightly, it makes a loud screeching sound, and you say "I would like to thank God for bringing me to this point in my life."

For every good deed, there is a hospitable gesture that should follow and that is thank you. More often than ever, it is forgotten or mere words uttered hastily, out of habit, with no real sincerity behind them.

For our creator who has given us everything, life, love, peace, joy and all of our earthly possessions, where do we begin with our thanksgiving? After verbally expressing our thanks, prayers of thankfulness are always a good place to begin. We connect with God when we pray. God's Word even tells us how to pray. In *Matthew 6:5-13*, there are specific instructions on where to pray and how to pray. God instructs us to go to our secret closet pray and he will reward us openly.

We can also thank God by honoring him with our lives. If we take our life and live it in a holy and righteous manner and keep Gods commandments, that would certainly be saying, "thank you God, I appreciate you."

Another way that we can thank God is with worship, praise and song. It is the least we can do for all that he has done, is still doing, and will do for us. We should each have a church home that we are supporting with our time, tithes and offerings.

Praise ye the Lord. Praise God in His sanctuary: Praise Him in the firmament of his power. 2 Praise Him for his mighty acts: Praise Him according to his excellent greatness: 3 Praise Him with the sound of the trumpet: praise Him with the psaltery and harp. 4 Praise Him with the timbrel and dance: Praise Him with the string instruments and organs. 5 Praise Him upon the loud cymbals: praise Him upon the high sounding cymbals. 6 Let every thing that hath breath praise the Lord. Praise ye the Lord.
    (Psalm 150:1-6)

Praise the Lord with song. Praise ye the Lord. Sing unto the Lord a new song, and his praise in the congregation of saints.
    (Psalm 149: 1)
Thank you Lord for everything.

We should also thank those individuals who helped us to get to where we are. These people may have helped to open doors that otherwise, would have been closed. They believed in us when no one else would. They encouraged us to not give up. They walked, the sometimes, difficult path to self-discovery along with us, and held our hand.

Conclusion

As you can see, life is full with the rich blessings of God. We each have but to realize, perfect and utilize our own true talents. We must pull together all of our resources. Our faith in God, our time, talents, strength and love must mesh together to bring about a wonderful end.

Through my experiences, I have learned that nothing worthwhile in life comes easy. We must sometimes go through the valleys of life to get to those mountain top experiences. The consolation, comes with the dawning of each new day, because with that new day comes another chance. It is one more day to be better than you were yesterday. It is one more day to please and glorify God. It is one more day to try and get life right. Therefore, press on when the going gets rough. Keep moving when you feel too weak to move. Then, allow the Holy Spirit to take over you and use each hour as if it is your last. Seize the moment, leaving a trail of beaten paths of blessings for others to follow.

Like many of you, I had been in search of my God given talents. I thank God for allowing me to realize them. It is my hope that he has guided my pen to help you in discovering, what has been yours all along. Through these words, I pray that you have gained knowledge of what your talents are, how they are to be used, as well as acquiring a taste for righteousness that you will want to savor.

In no way do I profess to know what God's plan is for someone with a particular skill or talent. However, I do reasonably believe that these beams of light that I have chosen to call talents did not come by chance. These rays of hope do not appear in our lives to remain un-nurtured. Neither are these gifts, given to collect dust on the shelves of life.

Pastor William Hunter Crews of the Greater Shiloh Baptist Church of Detroit, Michigan often said, "God has given everybody something to win with. What will you do with what he has given to you?" His encouraging words helped more than he knows, and will be forever etched in my mind. It is then our duty to take our God given talents and use them to glorify the Lord. In doing so, may we find purpose and God's plan for our life. May the peace of God be with you.

The End

Table 1.1 Train At Home -College Contacts

Thomas Edison State College
(888) 442-8372
http://www.tesc.edu

Regents College
http://www.regents.edu
(518) 464-8500

University Of Phoenix Online
(800) 366-9699
3201 E. Elwood Street
Phoenix, AZ 85034

National Commission for Cooperative Education
(617) 373-3770
http://www.co-op.edu

Education Direct
P.O. Box 1900
Scranton, PA 18501
(800) 275-4410
http://www.educationdir.com

Distance Education and Training Council: http:// www.detc.org

 Online Education: http://www.caso.com

California College For Health Sciences Online Education
2423 Hoover Avenue www.caso.com
National City, California 91950
(619) 477-4800
http://www.cchs.edu

Table 1.2-COLLEGE DIRECTORY

Alabama

Alabama A&M University
Alabama State University
Auburn University
Auburn University-Montgomery
Birmingham-Southern College
Concordia College
Faulkner University
Huntingdon College
Jacksonville State University
Judson College
Miles College
Oakwood College
Samford University
Spring Hill College
Stillman College
Talladega College
Troy State University-Dothan
Troy State University-Troy
Tuskegee University
University of Alabama
University of Alabama-Birmingham
University of Alabama-Huntsville
University of Mobile
University of Montevallo
University of North Alabama
University of South Alabama
University of West Alabama

Alaska

Alaska Pacific University
Sheldon Jackson College
University of Alaska-Anchorage
University of Alaska-Fairbanks
University of Alaska-Southeast

Arizona

Arizona State University
Grand Canyon University
Prescott College
University of Arizona
Western International University

Arkansas

Arkansas Baptist College
Arkansas State University
Arkansas Tech University
Harding University
Henderson State University
Hendrix College
John Brown University
Lyon College
Ouachita Baptist University
Philander Smith College
University of Arkansas
University of Arkansas-Little Rock
University of Arkansas-Monticello
University of Arkansas-Pine Bluff

University of Central Arkansas
University of the Ozarks
Williams Baptist College

California

Art Center College of Design
Azusa Pacific University
Bethany College
California Baptist University
California College of Arts and Crafts
California Institute of Technology
California Institute of the Arts
California Lutheran University
California State Poly. University-Pomona
California State University-Bakersfield
California State University-Chico
California State University-Dominguez Hills
California State University-Fresno
California State University-Fullerton
California State University-Hayward
California State University-Long Beach
California State University-Los Angeles
California State University-Northridge
California State University-Sacramento
California State University-San Bernardino
California State University-San Marcos
California State University-Stanislaus
California University of Pennsylvania
Cal Poly-San Luis Obispo
Chapman University
Christian Heritage College
Claremont McKenna College
Concordia University

Dominican University of California
Fresno Pacific University
Golden Gate University
Harvey Mudd College
Holy Names College
Hope International University
Humboldt State University
Humphreys College
John F. Kennedy University
La Sierra University
Loyola Marymount University
Master's Col. And Seminary
Menlo College
Miles College
Mount St. Mary's College
National University
New College of California
Notre Dame de Namur University
Occidental College
Otis Col. Of Art and Design
Pacific Union College
Pattern College
Pepperdine University
Pitzer College
Point Loma Nazarene University
Pomona College
San Diego State University
San Francisco Art Institute
San Francisco Conservatory of Music
San Francisco State University
San Jose State University
Santa Clara University
Simpson College
Sonoma State University
Southern California Institute of Architecture

Stanford University
St. Mary's College of California
Thomas Aquinas College
United States International University
University of California-Berkeley
University of California-Davis
University of California-Irvine
University of California-Los Angeles
University of California-Riverside
University of California-San Diego
University of California-Santa Barbara
University of California-Santa Cruz
University of Judaism
University of La Verne
University of the Pacific
Vanguard University of Southern California
Westmont College
Whittier College
Woodbury University

Colorado

Adams State College
Colorado Christian University
Colorado College
Colorado School of Mines
Colorado State University
Fort Lewis College
Mesa State College
Regis University
United States Air Force Academy
University of Colorado-Boulder
University of Colorado-Colorado Springs
University of Southern Colorado

REALIZING YOUR GOD GIVEN TALENTS

Western State College of Colorado

Connecticut

Albertus Magnus College
Connecticut College
Fairfield University
Quinnipiac University
Sacred Heart University
St. Joseph College
Teikyo Post University
Trinity College
United States Coast Guard Academy
University of Bridgeport
University of Hartford
University of New Haven
Wesleyan University
Western Connecticut State University
Yale University

Delaware

Delaware State University
Goldey Beacom College
University of Delaware
Wesley College
Wilmington College

District of Columbia (DC)

American University

Catholic University of America
Corcoran College of Art and Design
Gallaudet University
Georgetown University
George Washington University
Howard University
Southeastern University
Trinity College
University of District of Columbia

Florida

Barry University
Bethune-Cookman College
Clearwater Christian College
Eckerd College
Edward Waters College
Embry Riddle Aeronautical University
Flagler College
Florida A&M University
Florida Atlantic University
Florida Gulf Coast University
Florida Institute of Technology
Florida International University
Florida Memorial College
Florida Southern College
Florida State University
International College
Jacksonville University
Lynn University
Nova Southeastern University
Palm Beach Atlantic College
Ringling School of Art and Design
Rollins College

Stetson University
St. Leo University
St. Thomas University
University of Central Florida
University of Florida
University of Miami
University of North Florida
University of Tampa
University of West Florida
Warner Southern College
Webber College

Georgia

Agnes Scott College
Albany State University
Armstrong Atlantic State University
Augusta State University
Berry College
Brenau University
Brewton-Parker College
Clayton College and State University
Columbus State University
Covenant College
Emmanuel College
Emory University
Fort Valley State University
Georgia College and State University
Georgia Institute of Technology
Kennesaw State University
LaGrange College
Mercer University
Morehouse College
Morris Brown College
North Georgia College and State University

Oglethorpe University
Paine College
Piedmont College
Reinhardt College
Savannah College of Art and Design
Savannah State University
Shorter College
Southern Polytechnic State University
Spelman College
State University of West Georgia
Thomas University
Toccoa Falls College
University of Georgia
Valdosta State University]
Wesleyan College

Hawaii

Brigham Young University
Chaminade University of Honolulu
Hawaii Pacific University
University Of Hawaii-Hilo
University of Hawaii-Manoa

Idaho

Albertson College
Idaho State University
Northwest Nazarene University
University of Idaho

Illinois

Augustana College
Aurora University
Barat College
Benedictine University
Blackburn College
Bradley University
Columbia College
Concordia University-River Forest
DePaul University
Dominican University
Eastern Illinois University
East-West University
Elmhurst College
Eureka College
Greenville College
Illinois College
Illinois Institute of Technology
Illinois State University
Illinois Wesleyan University
Judson College
Kendall College
Knox College
Lake Forest College
Lewis University
MacMurray College
McKendree College
Millikin University
Monmouth College
National-Louis University
North Central College
Northeastern Illinois University
Northern Illinois University
North Central College
Northeastern Illinois University
Northern Illinois University

Northwestern University
Olivet Nazarene University
Principia College
Quincy University
Robert Morris College
Rockford College
Roosevelt University
Shimer College
Southern Illinois University-Carbondale
Southern Illinois University-Edwardsville
St Xavier University
Trinity Christian College
University of Illinois-Chicago
University of Illinois-Champaign
University of St. Francis
VanderCook College of Music
Wheaton College

Iowa

Briar Cliff College
Buena Vista University
Central College
Clarke College
Coe College
Cornell College
Dordt College
Drake University
Graceland University
Grand View College
Grinnell College
Iowa State University
Iowa Wesleyan College
Loras College
Luther College

Maharishi University of Management
Marycrest International University
Morningside College
Mount Mercy College
Mount St. Clare College
Northwestern College
St. Ambrose University
University of Dubuque
University of Iowa
University of Northern Iowa
Waldorf College
Wartburg College
William Penn University

Kansas

Baker University
Benedictine College
Bethany College
Bethel College
Central Christian College
Emporia State University
Fort Hays State University
Friends University
Kansas State University
Kansas Wesleyan University
McPherson College
Mid America Nazarene College
Newman University
Ottawa University
Pittsburg State University
Southwestern College
Sterling College
St. Mary College
Tabor College

University of Kansas
Washburn University
Wichita State University

Kentucky

Alice Lloyd College
Asbury College
Bellarmine University
Berea College
Brescia University
Campbellsville University
Centre College
Cumberland College
Georgetown College
Kentucky Christian College
Kentucky State University
Kentucky Wesleyan College
Lindsey Wilson College
Mid-Continent College
Midway College
Morehead State University
Murray State University
Pikeville College
Spalding University
Thomas More College
Transylvania University
University of Kentucky
University of Louisville
Western Kentucky University

Louisiana

Centenary College of Louisiana

Dillard University
Grambling State University
Louisiana College
Louisiana State University-Shreveport
Louisiana Tech University
Loyola University New Orlean
Nicholls State University
Northwestern State University of Louisiana
Our Lady of Holy Cross College
Southern University and A&M College
Southern University-New Orleans
Tulane University
University of Louisiana-Lafayette
University of Louisiana-Monroe
Xavier University of Louisiana

Maine

Bates College
Bowdoin College
Colby College
College of the Atlantic
Husson College
Maine College of Art
St. Joseph's College
Thomas College
Unity College
University of Maine-Augusta
University of Maine-Farmington
University of Maine-Fort Kent
University of Maine-Machias
University of Maine-Orono
University of Maine-Presque Isle
University of New England

University of Southern Maine

Maryland

Bowie State University
Capital college
College of Notre Dame of Maryland
Columbia Union College
Coppin State College
Frostburg University
Goucher College
Hood College
Johns Hopkins University
Loyola College
Maryland Institute College of Art
Morgan State University
Mount St. Mary's College
Salisbury University
St. John's College
St. Mary's College of Maryland
Towson University
University of Maryland-Baltimore County
University of Maryland-College Park
University of Maryland-Eastern Shore
University of Maryland-University College
Villa Julie College
Washington College
Western Maryland College

Massachusetts

American International College
Amherst College
Anna Maria College
Assumption College

Atlantic Union College
Babson College
Bay Path College
Becker College
Bentley College
Berklee College of Music
Brandeis University
Bridgewater State College
Clark University
College of the Holy Cross
Curry College
Eastern Nazarene College
Elms College
Emerson College
Emmanuel College
Endicott College
Fitchburg State College
Framingham State College
Franklin Institute
Gordon College
Hampshire College
Harvard University
Lasell College
Lesley College
Longy School of Music
Massachusetts College of Art
Massachusetts College of Liberal Arts
Massachusetts Institute of Technology
Merrimack College
Montserrat College of Art
Mount Holyoke College
Mount Ida College
New England Conservatory of Music
Nichols College
Northeastern University

Pine Manor College
Regis College
Salem State College
Simmons College
Simon's Rock College of Bard
Smith College
Springfield College
Stonehill College
Suffolk University
Tufts University
University of Massachusetts-Amherst
University of Massachusetts-Boston
University of Massachusetts-Dartmouth
University of Massachusetts-Lowell
Wellesley College
Wentworth Institute of Technology
Western New England College
Westfield State College
Wheaton College
Wheelock College
Williams College
Worcester Polytechnic Institute
Worcester State College

Michigan

Adrian College
Albion College
Alma College
Andrews University
Aquinas College
Baker College of Flint
Calvin College
Center For Creative Studies
Cleary College

Concordia College
Cornerstone University
Davenport College of Business
Davenport University-Eastern Regions
Eastern Michigan University
Ferris State University
Grand Valley State University
Hillsdale College
Hope College
Kalamazoo College
Kettering University
Lake Superior State University
Lawrence Technological University
Madonna University
Marygrove College
Michigan State University
Michigan Technological University
Northwood University
Oakland University
Olivet College
Rochester College
Saginaw Valley State University
Siena Heights University
Spring Arbor University
St. Mary's College
University of Michigan-Ann Arbor
University of Michigan-Dearborn
University of Michigan-Flint
Walsh College of Accounting and Business Administration
Wayne County Community College
Wayne State University
William Tyndale College

Minnesota

Augsburg College
Bemidji State University
Bethel College
Carleton College
College of St. Benedict
College of St. Catherine
College of St. Scholastica
College of Visual Arts
Concordia College-Moorhead
Concordia University-St. Paul
Crown College
Gustavus Adolphus College
Hamline University
MaCalester College
Metropolitan State University
Minnesota State University-Mankato
Minnesota State University-Moorhead
Northwestern College
Southwest State University
St. Cloud State University
St. John's University
St. Mary's University of Minnesota
St. Olaf College
University of Minnesota-Crookston
University of Minnesota-Duluth
University of Minnesota-Morris
University of Minnesota-Twin Cities
University of St. Thomas
Winona State University

Mississippi

Alcorn State University
Belhaven College
Blue Mountain College

Delta State University
Jackson State University
Milsaps College
Mississippi College
Mississippi State University
Mississippi University for Women
Mississippi Valley State University
Rust College
Tougaloo College
University of Mississippi
University of Southern Mississippi
William Carey College

Missouri

Avila College
Central Methodist College
Central Missouri State University
College of the Ozarks
Columbia College
Culver-Stockton College
Drury University
Evangel College
Fontbonne College
Hannibal LaGrange College
Kansas City Art Institute
Lincoln University
Lindenwood University
Maryville University of St. Louis
Missouri Baptist College
Missouri Southern State College
Missouri Valley College
Missouri Western State College
Northwest Missouri State University
Park University

Rockhurst University
Southeast Missouri State University
Southwest Baptist University
Southwest Missouri State University
Stephens College
Truman State University
University of Missouri-Columbia
University of Missouri-Kansas City
University of Missouri-Rolla
University of Missouri-St Louis
Webster University
Westminster College
William Jewell College
William Woods University

Montana

Carroll College
Montana State University-Billings
Montana State University-Bozeman
Montana State University-Northern
Montana Tech of the University of Montana
Rocky Mountain College
University of Great Falls
University of Montana

Nebraska

Bellevue University
Chadron State College
College of St. Mary
Concordia University

Creighton University
Dana College
Doane College
Grace University
Hastings College
Midland Lutheran College
Nebraska Wesleyan University
Peru State College
Union College
University of Nebraska-Kearney
University of Nebraska-Lincoln
University of Nebraska-Omaha
Wayne State College
York College

Nevada

Sierra Nevada College
University of Nevada-Las Vegas
University of Nevada-Reno

New Hampshire

Colby-Sawyer College
College for Lifelong Learning
Daniel Webster College
Dartmouth College
Franklin Pierce College
Keene State College
New England College
Notre Dame College
Plymouth State College
Southern New Hampshire University

St. Anselm College
University of New Hampshire

New Mexico

College of Santa Fe
College of the Southwest
New Mexico State University
St. John's College
University of New Mexico
Western New Mexico University

New York

Adelphi University
Alfred University
Bard College
Barnard College
Boricua College
Buffalo State College
Canisius College
Cazenovia College
Clarkson University
Colgate University
College of Aeronautics
College of Mount St. Vincent
College of New Rochelle
College of St. Rose
Columbia University
Concordia College
Cooper Union
Cornell University
CUNY-Baruch College
CUNY-Brooklyn College

REALIZING YOUR GOD GIVEN TALENTS

CUNY-City College
CUNY-College Staten Island
CUNY-Hunter College
CUNY-Lehman College
CUNY-Medgar Evers College
CUNY-New York Technical College
CUNY-Queens College
CUNY-York College
Daemen College
Dominican College of Blauvelt
Dowling College
Elmira College
Excelsior College
Fashion Institute of Technology
Fordham University
Hamilton College
Hartwick College
Hilbert College
Hobart and William Smith College
Hofstra University
Houghton College
Iona College
Ithaca College
Juilliard School
Keuka College
LeMoyne College
Long Island University-Brooklyn
Long Island University-Southampton College
Manhattan College
Manhattanville College
Marist College
Marymount College-Tarrytown
Marymount Manhattan College
Medaille College
Mercy College

Molloy College
Mount St. Mary College
Nazareth College of Rochester
New School University
New York Institute of Technology
New York University
Niagara University
Nyack College
Pace University
Polytechnic University
Pratt Institute
Rensselaer Polytechnic Institute
Roberts Wesleyan College
Russell Sage College
Sarah Lawrence College
Siena College
Skidmore College
St. Bonaventure University
St. Francis College
St. John Fisher College
St. John's University
St. Joseph's College
St. Lawrence University
St. Thomas Aquinas College
SUNY-Albany
SUNY-Binghamton
SUNY College-Cortland
SUNY College Environmental Science and Forestry
SUNY College-Fredonia
SUNY College of A & T-Cobleskill
SUNY College Arts & Sciences-Geneseo
SUNY College Arts & Sciences-New Paltz
SUNY College-Old Westbury
SUNY College-Oneonta
SUNY College-Potsdam

SUNY-Empire State College
SUNY-Farmingdale
SUNY-Oswego
SUNY-Plattsburgh
SUNY-Purchase College
SUNY-Stony Brook
SUNY-University at Buffalo
Syracruse University
Touro College
Union College
University of Rochester
Utica College of Syracuse University
Vassar College
Wagner College
Webb Institute
Wells College
Yeshiva University

North Carolina

Appalachian State University
Barton College
Belmont Abbey College
Bennett College
Brevard College
Campbell University
Catawba College
Chowan College
Davidson College
Duke University
East Carolina University
Elizabeth City State University
Elon University
Fayetteville State University
Gardner-Webb University

Greensboro College
Guilford College
High Point University
Johnson C. Smith University
Lees-McRae College
Lenoir-Rhyne College
Livingstone College
Mars Hill College
Meredith College
Methodist College
Montreat College
Mount Olive College
Peace College
Pfeiffer University
Queens College
Salem College
Shaw University
St. Andrews Presbyterian College
St. Augustine's College
University of North Carolina-Asheville
University of North Carolina-Chapel Hill
University of North Carolina-Charlotte
University of North Carolina-Greensboro
University of North Carolina-Pembroke
University of North Carolina-Wilmington
Wake Forest University
Warren Wilson College
Western Carolina University
Wingate University
Winston-Salem State University

North Dakota

Dickinson State University
Jamestown College

Mayville State University
Minot State University
North Dakota State University
University of North Dakota
Valley City State University

Ohio

Antioch College
Ashland University
Baldwin-Wallace College
Bluffton College
Bowling Green State University
Capital University
Case Western Reserve University
Cedarville University
Central State University
College of Mount St. Joseph
College of Wooster
Columbus College of Art and Design
David N, Myers College
Defiance College
Denison University
Franciscan University of Steubenville
Franklin University
Heidelberg College
Hiram College
John Carroll University
Kent State University
Kenyon College
Lake Erie College
Lourdes College
Malone College
Marietta College
Miami University-Oxford

Mount Union College
Mount Vernon Nazarene College
Muskingum College
Notre Dame College of Ohio
Oberlin College
Ohio Dominican College
Ohio Northern University
Ohio State University-Columbus
Ohio University
Ohio Wesleyan University
Otterbein College
Shawnee State University
Tiffin University
Union Institute
University of Akron
University of Dayton
University of Findlay
University of Rio Grande
University of Toledo
Urbana University
Ursuline College
Walsh University
Wilberforce University
Wilmington College
Wittenberg University
Wright State University
Xavier University
Youngstown State University

Oklahoma

Bartlesville Wesleyan College
Cameron University
East Central University
Langston University
Northeastern State University

Oklahoma Baptist University
Oklahoma Christian University
Oklahoma City University
Oklahoma Panhandle State University
Oklahoma State University
Oral Roberts University
Southern Nazarene University
St. Gregory's University
University of Oklahoma
University of Tulsa

Oregon

Concordia University
George Fox University
Lewis and Clark College
Linfield College
Marylhurst University
Northwest Christian College
Oregon Institute of Technology
Oregon State University
Pacific Northwest College of Art
Pacific University
Portland state University
Reed College
South Oregon University
University of Oregon
University of Portland
Warner Pacific College
Western Baptist College
Western Oregon University
Willamette University

Pennsylvania

Albright College
Allegheny College
Alvernia College
Arcadia University
Bloomsburg University of Pennsylvania
Bryn Athyn College
Bryn Mawr College
Bucknell University
Cabrini College
Carnegie Mellon University
Cedar Crest College
Chatham College
Chestnut Hill College
Cheyney University of Pennsylvania
Clarion University
College Misericordia
Curtis Institute of Music
Delaware Valley College
Desales University
Dickinson College
Drexel University
Duquesne University
Eastern College
East Stroudsburg University of Pennsylvania
Edinboro University of Pennsylvania
Elizabethtown College
Franklin and Marshall College
Gannon University
Geneva College
Gettysburg College
Gratz College
Grove City College
Gwynedd-Mercy College
Haverford College

Holy Family College
Immaculata College
Indiana University of Pennsylvania
Juniata College
King's College
Kutztown University of Pennsylvania
Lafayette College
La Roche College
La Salle University
Lebanon Valley College
Lehigh University
Lincoln University
Lock Haven University of Pennsylvania
Lycoming College
Mansfield University of Pennsylvania
Marywood University
MCP Hahnemann University
Mercyhurst College
Messiah College
Millersville University of Pennsylvania
Moore College of Art and Design
Moravian College
Mount Aloysius College
Muhlenberg College
Neumann College
Pennsylvania College of Technology
Penn State-Erie, Behrend College
Pennsylvania State University-University Park
Philadelphia University
Point Park College
Robert Morris College
Rosemont College
Seton Hill College
Shippensburg University of Pennsylvania
Slippery Rock University of Pennsylvania

St. Francis University
St. Joseph's University
St. Vincent College
Susquehanna University
Swarthmore College
Temple University
Thiel College
University of Pennsylvania
University of Scranton
University of the Arts
Ursinus College
Villanova University
Washington and Jefferson College
Waynesburg College
Westchester University of Pennsylvania
Westminster College
Widener University
Wilkes University
Wilson College
York college of Pennsylvania

Rhode Island

Brown University
Bryant College
Johnson and Wales University
Providence College
Rhode Island College
Rhode Island School of Design
Roger Williams University
Salve Regina University
University of Rhode Island

South Carolina

Allen University
Anderson College
Benedict College
Charleston Southern University
The Citadel
Claflin University
Clemson University
Coastal Carolina University
College of Charleston
Coker College
Columbia College
Converse College
Erskine College
Francis Marion University
Furman University
Lander University
Limestone College
Morris College
Newberry College
North Greenville College
Presbyterian College
South Carolina State University
Southern Wesleyan University
University of South Carolina-Aiken
University of South Carolina-Columbia
University of South Carolina-Spartanburg
Voorhees College
Winthrop University
Wofford College

South Dakota

Augustana College
Black Hills State University

Dakota State University
Dakota Wesleyan University
Mount Marty College
Northern State University
South Dakota School of Mines and Technology
South Dakota State University
University of South Dakota

Tennessee

Austin Peay State University
Belmont University
Bethel College
Bryan College
Carson-Newman College
Christian Brothers University
Crichton College
Cumberland College
David Lipscomb University
East Tennessee State University
Fisk University
Freed-Hardeman University
King College
Lambuth University
Lane College
Lee University
Le Moyne-Owen College
Lincoln Memorial University
Martin Methodist College
Maryville College
Middle Tennessee State University
Milligan College
Rhodes College
Southern Adventist University
Tennessee State University

Tennessee Technological University
Tennessee Wesleyan College
Trevecca Nazarene University
Tusculum College
Union University
University of Tennessee-Chattanooga
University of Tennessee-Knoxville
University of Tennessee-Martin
University of the South
Vanderbilt University

Texas

Abilene Christian University
Angelo State University
Austin College
Baylor University
Concordia University-Austin
Dallas Baptist University
Hardin-Simmons University
Howard Payne University
Huston-Tillotson College
Jarvis Christian College
Lamar University
LeTourneau University
Lubbock Christian University
McMurry University
Midwestern State University
Our Lady of the Lake University
Paul Quinn College
Prairie View A&M University
Rice University
Sam Houston State University
Schreiner University
Southern Methodist University

Southwestern Adventist University
Southwestern University
Southwest Texas State University
St. Edward's University
Stephen F. Austin State University
Sul Ross State University
Tarleton State University
Texas A&M International University
Texas A&M University-College Station
Texas A&M University-Commerce
Texas A&M University-Corpus Christi
Texas A&M University-Galveston
Texas A&M University-Kingsville
Texas Christian University
Texas Lutheran University
Texas Southern University
Texas Tech University
Texas Wesleyan University
Texas Woman's University
Trinity University
University of Mary Hardin-Baylor
University of North Texas
University of St. Thomas
University of Texas-Arlington
University of Texas-Austin
University of Texas-Brownsville
University of Texas-Dallas
University of Texas-El Paso
University of Texas of the Permian Basin
University of Texas-Pan American
University of Texas-San Antonio
University of Texas-Tyler
University of the Incarnate Word
Wayland Baptist University
West Texas A&M University

Wiley College

Utah

Southern Utah University
University of Utah
Utah State University
Utah Valley State College
Weber State University
Westminster College

Vermont

Bennington College
Burlington College
Champlain College
College of St. Joseph
Goddard College
Green Mountain College
Johnson State College
Lyndon State College
Marlboro College
Middlebury College
Norwich University
Southern Vermont College
St. Michael's College
University of Vermont
Vermont Technical College

Virginia

Averette College
Bluefield College
Bridgewater College

Christendom College
Christopher Newport University
College of William and Mary
Eastern Mennonite University
Emory and Henry College
Ferrum College
George Mason University
Hampden-Sydney College
Hampton University
Hollins University
James Madison University
Marshall-Realizing Your God

Liberty University
Longwood College
Lynchburg College
Mary Baldwin College
Marymount University
Mary Washington College
Norfolk State University
Old Dominion University'
Radford University
Randolph-Macon College
Randolph-Macon Woman's College
Roanoke College
Shenandoah University
St. Paul's College
Sweet Briar College
University of Richmond
University of Virginia
University of Virginia-Wise
Virginia Commonwealth University
Virginia Intermont College
Virginia Military Institute
Virginia State University

Virginia Tech
Virginia Union University
Virginia Wesleyan College
Washington and Lee University

Wisconsin

Alverno College
Beloit College
Cardinal Stritch University
Carthage College
Concordia University Wisconsin
Edgewood College
Lakeland College
Lawrence University
Marian College of Fond du Lac
Marquette University
Mount Mary College
Mount Senerio College
Northland College
Ripon College
Silver Lake College
St. Norbert College
University of Wisconsin-Eau Claire
University of Wisconsin-Green Bay
University of Wisconsin-La Crosse
University of Wisconsin-Madison
University of Wisconsin-Milwaukee
University of Wisconsin-Oshkosh
University of Wisconsin-Parkside
University of Wisconsin-Plattesville
University of Wisconsin-River Falls
University of Wisconsin-Stevens Point
University of Wisconsin-Stout
University of Wisconsin-Superior

GEORGETTA MARSHALL

University of Wisconsin-Whitewater
Viterbo University
Wisconsin Lutheran University

Printed in the United States
1409700001B/148-198